Writing Memoir

Writing Memoir

tips from an editor on writing

life stories

Kathy Stewart

Writing Memoir: tips from an editor on writing life stories

Copyright © Kathy Stewart 2016

First published in 2016 by
Authors' Ally
www.authorsally.net
27 Wallaby Drive
Mudgeeraba, Qld, 4213
Australia

Stewart, Kathy
Writing Memoir: tips from an editor on writing life stories

1st edition

ISBN: 9780980815382

Biography--Authorship.
Genealogy--Authorship.

929.1072

About the Author

Kathy Stewart owns and runs an editing and appraisal service situated on the Gold Coast of Australia. She has always been passionate about writing and has worked as a professional editor since 2004. Many of the books she has worked on are now selling in bookstores and online and many others are in the pipeline. Her manuscripts, The Chameleon Factor and Race Against Time, were shortlisted and longlisted respectively for the 2010 Crime Writers Association Debut Dagger Award in the UK.

Contact Kathy at: kathystewart640@gmail.com

Other books by Kathy Stewart

Non-fiction:

Self-Editing Your Novel

Creative non-fiction:

The Armoured Train Incident

Fiction:

Novel:

Chameleon

Short story collections:

Over to You

Star Turn and Other Stories

Children's book:

Betty Bee's Garden Adventure (as Kathleen Stewart)

Contents

Introduction 1

What is a Life Story? 3

Why Write a Memoir? 14

What If I Hurt People? 22

Gathering Information 39

    Memory 39

        Lists 39

        Diaries and journals 43

        Photographs 44

        Mementos 45

        Meditation 46

        Consult family and friends 48

        Other aids for memory recall 49

    Research 51

        Internet and search engines 52

        Local libraries 54

        State, provincial or regional libraries 55

        National libraries 56

University libraries 58

Special-interest libraries 59

Historical societies 59

Archives 60

Books and bibliographies 71

Industry journals 72

Museums 72

Local publications 74

Genealogical societies 75

Cemeteries 75

Cautions 77

Conclusion 81

Getting Started 90

The Nuts and Bolts 109

Character files 109

Writing for traditional publication 110

Writing for other reasons 112

The writing process 113

How do I make my memoir interesting? 117

Follow the emotion 119

Storytelling principles 121

Overall structure 121

Components of storytelling 122

Dealing with writer's block 135

Tip..137

Publishing Methods 144

Traditional 144

Self-publishing 146

Print on demand 154

Blogs 155

Ebooks 157

Private 160

Audio books 161

Photo books 161

Making backups 165

Building a Family Tree 169

Conclusion 172

Acknowledgements 174

Useful Sites 175

For my family. Thanks for all your love and support.

Introduction

During my career as an editor, I've had a number of memoirs cross my desk. All of them, without fail, have left a lasting impression on me. I always felt I needed to be upfront with the authors, to warn them that they faced a tough journey if they wanted to be traditionally published, but most chose, very wisely, to ignore my advice. The result is that some have been traditionally published and some have chosen to self-publish. All have produced very readable, interesting and enlightening memoirs.

You can use this book in a number of ways.

If you've already written a memoir you can use it to check whether you have included some important points before publication, or you can use it as a blueprint for how to write a memoir for publication. If you have no intention of publishing your memoir then you can follow the advice tailored specifically for you.

Whichever category you fall into, I hope you will find this book helpful.

What is a Life Story?

Life stories can take many forms, so do you know the difference between writing an autobiography, your memoirs, a memoir, a biography, or a family history?

An **autobiography** is the story of your whole life, from birth to where you are now.

Memoirs are usually written by famous or infamous people, for example, Winston Churchill, the famous Prime Minister of Great Britain, or perhaps Ronald Biggs, one of the infamous perpetrators of the Great Train Robbery. Or, more recently, Frank Abagnale, former conman, cheque-forger and impostor turned FBI agent who was the star of the book and later the movie, *Catch Me If You*

Can. Quite often the memoirs focus on only one period of interest to the world at large. In Winston Churchill's case this might well be the Second World War, or it could be the part he played as a journalist in the Anglo-Boer War. The point is that it focuses on a period that is of particular interest to most people.

A **memoir** contains selected incidents from a person's life that illustrate a theme. It's a personal account of events in your life given from your perspective. So you might like to focus on only one aspect of your life. You might have been a keen sailor in your day, and visited many interesting places. You might be an excellent cook who would like to pass on recipes as well as tales about where these recipes came from. You might have had an interesting or deprived childhood, been born in an unusual or turbulent place, or during an interesting period in history.

As you can see, there are many different foci for a memoir and it's up to you to choose which aspect or aspects of your life you'd like to highlight. This is wonderful news, because it means you can be selective about what you choose to reveal.

To me, this point is also the key to writing memoir: you reveal only those incidents which illustrate your theme.

Biography is an account of a person's life written by someone else.

Family history, otherwise often referred to as genealogy, is the study of families, including the tracing of their lineages and histories. These histories are often written up using charts and narrative, thereby preserving accurate records of a family.

At times there is a blurring of these definitions, so what might start as a biography, an account of the life of your grandmother who ran a hospital in a remote region, might morph into a memoir as you explore the influences your grandmother had over you and the life lessons you learnt from her.

A family history might also turn into a biography if you find that one character is more interesting than others, and that his or her life story begins to take over the narrative.

Although I will concentrate on memoir in this book, much of what I've written also applies to other types of life stories.

Summary

- **Autobiography:** the story of your whole life, from birth to where you are now.
- **Memoirs:** usually written by famous or infamous people and only focuses on one period of interest to the world at large.
- **Memoir:** selected incidents from your own life which illustrate a theme.
- **Biography:** an account of a person's life written by someone else.
- **Family history:** the study of genealogy, including lineages and history.

Writing exercise 1:

Write at least half a page starting with the words 'The thing I most want to write about is ...'

Writing exercise 2:

Read the following excerpt:

As it became obvious that Mark was not improving, Rod gave up on the exercise routine. The water level dropped and soon dried up, causing the pool to crack. Rod began to use it for compost.

'Mark needs an interest,' he said to Betty and he brought home a pellet gun. 'I'll teach you to shoot,' he told Mark. And Mark became fanatical, spending most of each day aiming at and downing any bird he spied. Mom was concerned about Henry. Since Mark had discovered shooting, Henry had gone AWOL, either frightened off by the noise or killed by one of Mark's pellets.

We were playing in our village, now back behind the tank after the debacle with Shay, when we heard the 'pop' as a shot was fired from Mark's pellet gun.

Accustomed to it by now, we carried on playing, hating the senseless killing.

'Margaret, fetch that dove.' Mark's voice was shrill with excitement. 'There, you fool. There, behind that bush.'

We stood up and looked over the fence. Margaret emerged, carrying a struggling grey dove, its chest covered in blood. Its beak opened spasmodically as it gasped for air. We watched as Margaret carried the bird to where Mark sat in his wheelchair. His back was to us. Uneasy, we resumed our play.

'Fetch me a knife, you bitch,' Mark ordered.

Abby and Pam were sitting on the back steps in the sun, watching the play unfold. Abby told us later that Margaret emerged from the kitchen, carrying a sharp knife. Mark took it and turned the bird over, exposing its mutilated chest and heaving sides.

Abby screamed, a bloodcurdling, ear-splitting yell.

'Noooo.' She sounded as though she was in pain.

The animal fear of it made us stop in our tracks. Not normally athletic, Anne vaulted the fence and began to run to Abby's side. The little girl was sobbing, her dirty face streaked with tears. Mark laughed, his hands bloody. Pam watched Anne approaching, a vacant expression on her face.

'What're you scared of, you idiot?' he shrieked, laughing at Abby, until he saw Anne looming near. Fear crossed his face and then bravado took over.

'Look!' he said, holding the injured bird for Anne to inspect.

He'd made an incision in its chest cavity and exposed the still-beating heart. The little bird fluttered in his grasp, its eyes glazing over with pain, the membranes half closing its eyes as it breathed its last.

'You monster!' Anne screamed. 'You disgusting pervert!' She made a lunge for the bird, but Mark pulled his hands close in to his body.

'Leave it! It's mine!' he shrieked, and laughed maniacally. The little bird lay limp in his hand. Anne could see that it had died. 'Get out of my yard,' Mark ordered. 'Margaret, tell this bitch to go or I'll report you to my dad. He'll sack you.'

Margaret looked at Anne with frightened eyes.

'Don't worry, Margaret, I'll go, but you're a disgusting cruel little toad, Mark. You shouldn't have a pellet gun.' Anne turned to leave.

'Stupid bitch,' Mark sneered. 'Don't you speak to me like that. I'll tell my dad on you. Yaah, run away. Cow. Pig!' he screamed at Anne's departing back.

Abby ran after Anne and clutched onto her hand. Anne looked down into Abby's tear-streaked face. Abby gazed back through solemn blue eyes, sucking her thumb vigorously.

'Do you want to come and play with Jess?' Anne asked.

Abby nodded, still sucking her thumb.

'What about Pam?' Anne asked.

Pam waddled over to Margaret and flung her arms around Margaret's smooth brown legs. Anne lifted Abby over the fence.

'I'll tell Dad, you little cow,' Mark yelled after Abby. 'I'll tell him you pinched me!'

Abby removed her thumb from her mouth and covered her ears. She ran into our kitchen.

'Take her to your room, Jess. Let her play with your toys,' Anne said.

Disappointed at abandoning our game in our village, I complied, but Abby was in no mood to play. She sat on the bed, looking miserable.

'Come, Abby,' I said. 'Would you like to play with my horses?' I showed her the stuffed horses we'd made from Dad's old socks and some sucker sticks. We were immensely proud of them. Abby shook her head.

'Would you like to colour in?'

Again, she shook her head.

'Let me brush your hair then. Would you like that?' I volunteered.

Abby nodded emphatically and I fetched a brush from my cupboard. Her platinum blonde hair was matted and dull and so tangled I was afraid I would hurt her as I tried to brush out the knots. She sat as though mesmerized, obviously enjoying the experience, and her hands grew still in her lap as she watched me brushing her hair in the mirror.

'Abby, Abby!' Betty was calling over the fence.

Eunice came through to the bedroom, where Anne, Mary and I were talking to Abby while we all coloured in pictures in various books our aunt had provided.

'Mrs David is calling for Abby,' she said. 'Come Abby, I'll help you over the fence.' Eunice's voice was kind and she held her hand out to the little girl.

Abby stood up reluctantly, looking at each of us in turn, a silent plea in her eyes. We looked back, unable to offer any help. Abby followed Eunice through to the kitchen.

'You're in trouble, my girl.' Betty's voice drifted to us as we sat huddled on the floor in the bedroom. 'You wait till your father comes home. He'll spank you for hurting Mark.'

Later, we heard Abby's frightened screams. Mark, in his wheelchair outside the kitchen door, laughed. Pam and Shay stood outside, looking towards the house. Rod was obviously home.

Did you enjoy this piece?
If yes, then what did you enjoy about it?

If no, then what didn't you enjoy about it?

Write down what you can glean from this piece, for instance, who are the characters, how old are they, what are their social circumstances, what are they like, what are their likes and dislikes, what emotions do they feel, what is the relationship between the characters, what do you think might be happening, and where is this piece set? Go into plenty of detail and see how much you can surmise about the overall story.

Have you done that? Good. What I'd like you to take particular note of is how this author has set the scene, introduced dialogue and how she has handled the timeline.

Exercise 3:
Try writing a story from your own life emulating how this story has been told.

Why Write a Memoir?

There's no denying that as the baby-boomers age, it's becoming increasingly fashionable to write memoir in order to leave a lasting legacy to children and grandchildren. Is that wrong? No, of course not. It's a perfectly good reason, and one that no one could dispute.

To elaborate, though, what other reasons could there be?

Perhaps the first of these is in order to pass on knowledge or skills. This could be as simple as passing on favourite recipes or encompass more complex tasks such as how to build a jet engine. Passing on life skills is a really valid reason to write your memoir.

You may want to pass on your philosophy for life, to teach your descendants how to cope with problems. It is *your* solution.

A memoir could also be a way to pass on knowledge about family relationships, family secrets, family lore. Let's face it, legends about real people are as old as human history; it's how history was passed on from generation to generation. Just think of people like Count Dracula; or Lucrezia and Cesare Borgia; or Florence Nightingale; and what about the stories of King Arthur and his knights; the Knights Templar; or King Alfred and the burned cakes?

Which brings me to the next point.

Would you like to entertain? If you are a good raconteur and would like to keep people enthralled with a riveting tale or make people chuckle then this is an excellent reason to write your memoir. What could be better than leaving a legacy of laughter and fun?

Most people just want their family to understand how life was for them, to know what they thought, why they thought it, and what forces shaped their lives. They want to be understood and to pass on their life values to those they care about. So you could say you'd like to write your memoir to give your descendants a glimpse into your life, what you thought, felt, what you saw, the food you ate, the attitudes you developed.

Summary

The reasons to write a memoir can be summed up as follows:

- Passing on knowledge and skills
- Passing on family lore
- Passing on philosophy
- In order that your descendants will know, understand and appreciate you

Writing exercise 1:

Write at least half a page on 'The most tragic thing ...'

Writing exercise 2:

Read the following excerpt:

His father's death and Mum's new-found independence seemed to catapult Dad into an even worse mood. I don't know if it was the realization of his own mortality, whether he felt some type of guilt or he just plain resented Mum not being at his beck and call, but he drank even more heavily and, coupled with the effects of the head injury, had constant headaches, resulting in a perpetual bad mood. Mostly he was a loud, raging drunk, but occasionally he would come home in a sullen, quiet mood, seething with pent-up anger, and we learnt to fear these moods more than anything.

It was on one such day that he came home early from work. It was a Saturday and he'd done shift work. Mum was out visiting clients who could only be visited over the weekend, so she was unavailable to fetch Dad from 'work', meaning the pub.

It was a hot afternoon, blustery, with a dry wind blowing from the north. Dad had finished work, visited the pub and then, unable to raise Mum on the telephone, he'd had to *walk* home – a long way in the heat. He was spoiling for a fight, but when he came in, Mum was still out.

'Where's your mother?' he growled in a fierce, cold voice.

'She's working,' Les answered, her voice shaky.

Peter and I stayed in the background, watching warily.

'Where's my lunch?' Dad asked, glaring at us.

'I don't know,' said Les, insolence creeping into her voice. 'I don't think Mum was expecting you back for lunch – not at four o' clock, anyway.'

'What ...? You cheeky little bitch. You'd better make me some. *Raus.*' The German word was used to engender fear, evoke pictures of dominance. 'I expect it in ten minutes,' he challenged Les, provoking her, knowing cooking wasn't her forte.

'Make it yourself.' Les took the bait, incensed by his manner.

His rage boiled over. 'You bloody, useless, ugly —' He made a dive for Les, missing her as she ducked under his arm and reached for the door. We scampered through, running for our lives as he lumbered down the steps, surprisingly agile for someone so big and so drunk.

We ran towards the storeroom, ready to flee to the front of the house and out of the yard if need be, to wait until Mum came home or he pacified. But he didn't follow. Instead he turned the other way, and made his way with a fierce determination to the bottom of the yard, to Mum's vegetable garden and the fowl runs.

Relieved that he hadn't followed us, we huddled near the storeroom and heard the squawking as he neared the fowl runs. What was he up to?

He came back up the yard after several minutes, clutching a tiny, brown, feathered body in his huge hand, her head hanging limply to one side, her neck obviously broken – dead. It was Biddy.

19

A strangled cry escaped my lips and I rose, my instincts telling me to save her.

'She's dead,' whispered Les. 'She's dead, Jamie. He's killed her.' And they held me back as the tears streamed down my face.

Waiting for Mum to return, we plotted to leave home, Les and Peter on Les's bike, with me running alongside.

By the time Mum came back, the smell of roast chicken wafted from the kitchen. Unrepentant, Dad told us in great detail how Biddy had come up to him as he entered the run, before he'd seized her by the neck and broken it with a few savage twists. He ate her small, pathetic body with seeming relish, chewing the tiny bones and mopping up the gravy with thick hunks of bread.

We hated him with a passion.

Did you enjoy this piece?
If yes, then what did you enjoy about it?
If no, then what didn't you enjoy about it?

Write down what you can glean from this piece, such as who are the characters, how old are they, what are their social circumstances, what are they like, what are their likes and dislikes, what emotions do they feel, what is the relationship between the characters, what do you think might be happening, and where is this piece set? Go into plenty of detail and see how much you can surmise about the overall story.

Once you have done that, what I'd like you to note in the above piece is how this author has introduced the scene using a fairly long passage of narration, and then launched into dialogue.

Writing exercise 3:
Try writing a story from your own life emulating how this story has been told.

What If I Hurt People?

Is it worth alienating people?

Some stories just beg to be told and by telling them you could be helping others to come to terms with a difficult situation themselves, or inspire them to take steps that will dramatically improve their lives. However, telling your story can come at a cost to yourself and others that simply may not be worth it, and you need to be aware of this before embarking on a tell-all exposé.

Far be it from me to bridle you and prevent you from telling a story that needs to be told. Just temper your enthusiasm with realism and be aware of the pitfalls you might face.

Concern that you might hurt someone is a well-founded reason to be cautious. At writers' festivals I've attended, I've listened to many authors speak about the negative reaction to the memoir they've written.

By publishing your tell-all, you might find yourself alienated from family, friends, your community, and your work colleagues.

Does everything need to be told?

The first thing to mull over is whether everything needs to be told. If your uncle sexually abused you, the matter obviously does need to be dealt with, but perhaps a memoir is not the best place to do this.

You could consider writing about this incident as fiction rather than as fact.

Some might say this is the coward's way out, but is it really? If you did reveal everything about a particular incident, who stands to get hurt? You might, for one. You may be sued, or alienated from your support network, as mentioned earlier, but others such as your family, friends, and the broader community may also be hurt by your actions.

Settling a score

If you've had a particularly nasty experience at the hands of a parent, uncle, spouse, sibling or 'friend', you might be tempted to 'spill the beans' and get even with them via your memoir. Think carefully about this. Will the payoff be worth it? People's reactions are seldom predictable and your attempt to get back at someone may be misconstrued; you may hurt someone you had no intention of harming. People may think, erroneously, that the terrible lover you mock in your book is them, when in actual fact it is not them at all.

One author whose book I worked on found he was cut off by a female friend when his book was released, even though he'd not referred to her in the book at all. The point is that she thought he had, and she didn't like what she thought she read about herself, so she was upset.

Another 'friend' threatened to sue the same author over what he felt was libel. The libel case never came to anything, but the author lost a valued and long-term ally, and the relationship has never recovered.

Would you want this to happen with people you know? Is it worth it?

I quite often give talks on writing memoir at local libraries and find there are always some members of the audience who approach me afterwards to discuss writing their own memoir. Some are in the process, others are just thinking about it, but a common thread is that they would like their story to be told in order to get back at someone they feel has harmed them.

Let me say upfront that revenge is not a good motive for writing a memoir. While it may be tempting, there are so many points that militate against it.

Preferably resist the temptation to settle any scores and focus instead on the higher reason for telling your story, that is, although you may be recounting a story of how your mother's alcoholism affected you, you are also telling a story of human resilience, or whatever your particular case may be.

Portray other points of view

As most of us have an innate sense of fairness, your memoir is more likely to have wider appeal if you can give a balanced view of incidents that occurred, perhaps even giving the other person's point of view so readers can judge the merits for themselves.

Having said that, though, this is your memoir and you're the star, so you can really write it any way you like. It may be as well to take into account, though, that your memory of an event may not be as accurate as you think it is, or you may have misunderstood a situation, especially if you were young.

You can get around this point about differing memories by making it clear at the outset that the stories you are recounting are your version of events and they're taken from your memory, so they may not be all that accurate, although you believe they are.

In line with this aspect, preferably resist allowing too many family members to help you write your memoir. Because we all have differing opinions, if you try to please everyone you're likely to end up with a mish-mash that won't satisfy anyone.

The main thing to bear in mind is that we all have a point of view. None of us are exactly the same. If you asked a hundred people for their opinion on any particular subject, you'd probably get a hundred different answers. Granted, some would be similar, but they're unlikely to be carbon copies.

If someone in your past has injured you and you would like to write about it then perhaps start by trying to understand what shaped their life, what external and internal forces were at play, what makes them tick. Most people don't set out to be bad. Events in their lives have shaped them that way.

Remember too that even the worst people on Earth probably don't see themselves as bad. We always try to justify our actions.

Is there another way?

If you do decide to tell a story in your memoir that is likely to hurt someone, consider if there's another way to tell it.

Humour is often a good tool to defuse potentially hurtful situations, and self-deprecating humour, in particular, works really well. So while you're illustrating an event which could cause others to bristle, if you make yourself the star of the story and yourself the butt of the joke, they're more likely to laugh along with you – or at least smile and not sue you.

If you can't find it in yourself to tell the story in a humorous way, or if the subject matter clearly doesn't lend itself to humour, then perhaps try to tell it in a positive way, allowing the other person as much leeway as you can, that is, be as fair as you can. Remember: bitterness and self-pity are unattractive qualities and you won't come across well if you portray these in your memoir.

Fiction is another very effective way to handle tricky situations. Via fiction you can change the person's identity sufficiently that they are unrecognisable, but you can still deal with the issue. Even with fictionalising your memoir, though, there may still be some people who think they are mentioned in your work and take umbrage, but if you change enough about the situation, for example, the sex of the person, then this is less likely to happen.

A word of timely caution here is that if you decide to fictionalise only part of your memoir rather than the whole, then preferably state this somewhere in your blurb or in the front matter of your book, for example: some parts of this memoir have been fictionalised, or you could subtitle your book: a fictionalised memoir.

The main reason this would be done would be to change the names of people to protect their identity, and the facts would still be correct, but as long as you state that parts of the story are fiction that should absolve you from any angry backlash should your memoir become famous.

I think here of the James Frey case when it was discovered his memoir, *A Million Little Pieces*, had fiction in it. He had been interviewed by talk-show host Oprah Winfrey on the basis that the story was a factual account of his life and book sales had soared, so when it emerged his story was not entirely true, he had to issue an apology and the publisher had to offer to take back any books from dissatisfied readers.

Right of reply

Another point to keep in mind is that people have the right to reply to any accusations you level at them, so it could be interpreted as a low act if you pick on someone who is in no position to defend themselves, either because they have passed on or because they are ill, for instance with an age-related illness like Alzheimer's. Consider carefully whether you are being fair to people who have been in your life, and whether you have the right to trash their name to your descendants.

On the other hand, if your life has been shaped by something that a relative did then you do have the right to write this down and share the impact this had on your life. For instance you might have had a mother who was an alcoholic or was mentally ill; you might have had a brother or uncle who abused you; you might have had neglectful parents.

If you would like to write about how these circumstances affected you, then do so, but keep in mind that others have a right to state their case too; they have a right to dispute your telling of events.

Conclusion

Please remember, I'm not trying to discourage you from writing your memoir, rather just trying to point out the pitfalls and perhaps give you alternatives that will enable you to still pass on your life story without causing grief to others.

If, after you have considered all the above-mentioned ramifications, you do decide to tell your story about how these incidents affected you then

31

my suggestion is to employ some of the techniques mentioned earlier and tell of the incidents in the fairest way possible.

An example of what can transpire as a result of a published tell-all memoir is the story surrounding the brilliant but tragic book *A Child called "It"* by Dave Pelzer. Dave's purpose in telling his story was not to get back at his parents but rather to document how the human spirit can triumph over adversity. Dave's brother Richard has also written a memoir, *A Brother's Journey*, which confirms much of the abuse Dave claims happened to him, but there are others, family members included, who dispute Dave's recounting of events.

Dave has since written a number of other memoirs, one of which is *A Man named Dave: a story of Triumph and Forgiveness,* in which he forgives his father for the abuse he suffered.

It's as well to note both the negative and positive reactions to Dave's books. His retelling of events has helped innumerable people cope with similar situations themselves but has also brought him much retribution, which, in the light of his abuse as a child, must be hard to deal with.

However, if you can use your memoir to help others avoid the situation you found yourself in, and write about the party who injured you with humour, love or compassion, or all of those, then you probably have a valid reason for writing about the events you have in mind.

Summary

To summarise, before embarking on writing your memoir, perhaps ask yourself these questions:

- Is it worth alienating people?
- Does everything need to be told?
- Am I using this memoir to settle a score?
- Have I considered other points of view?
- Could I tell the story in another way?
- Have I been fair?
- Will the consequences be worth it?

Writing exercise 1:

Write at least half a page on 'I remember when ...'

Writing exercise 2:

Read the following excerpt:

I take out a copy of the official letter and pass it to Ephraim. He puts on his glasses and reads. I wait until he's finished and then talk him through the implications. It takes a while so we order more drinks. He doesn't ask any questions.

When I stop speaking he leans forward, sips his whiskey and says, 'I am pleased that he is still alive. At one stage, when I had not heard from him for a while, I thought he had been killed. I saw nothing in the newspapers and so thought he had been captured and executed. It is a great relief to receive word that he is alive and will face trial. It is a real coup for the security forces to capture someone like him.'

'He also thought he would be killed,' I say.

'He had a girlfriend there. There is no mention of her.' He lifts the letter from the table and replaces it with care.

'She wasn't in the country at the time of his arrest. She's safe,' I say.

'No.' He shakes his head. 'She wrote me to say she was going back in. I have heard nothing from her since then. I am worried about her.'

I promise to find out what has happened to her.

'How are Uri's spirits?' Ephraim changes the subject. 'Is he aware of what he is facing?'

'His morale is good. He's very calm. Each time I see him he seems strong.'

'Tell me how he was captured,' he says.

I reply that he doesn't know who informed on him. It may have been a colleague of his, but he's not sure. We hope it will emerge during the trial, although we know the State often keeps the identity of informants a secret. The circumstances of his arrest suggest he was betrayed. I consider the girlfriend, but don't voice my suspicions. I go into the details of his arrest.

Ephraim nods slowly and says, 'And that is what Uri told you?'

'Yes, it seems to me that his capture was more than just good luck or good police work. From the number of vehicles involved and the huge number of security police on the scene, it strikes me as a lot more than mere coincidence.'

We sit a while in silence. I watch Ephraim. He looks older than the last time I saw him. The stress is obviously telling on him. I decide he deserves to know the full score.

'After he was captured, he was interrogated and tortured. I think they wanted to show their citizens they'd caught a foreign spy. They wanted the credit and the international exposure. If he'd simply disappeared, that wouldn't have happened. He's worth more to them alive than dead. That could change, though. His usefulness could run its course. We have to act now – the sooner the better.'

Did you enjoy this piece?
If yes, then what did you enjoy about it?

If no, then what didn't you enjoy about it?

Write down what you can glean from this piece, such as who are the characters, how old are they, what are their social circumstances, what are they like, what are their likes and dislikes, what emotions do they feel, what is the relationship between the characters, what do you think might be happening, and where is this piece set? Go into plenty of detail and see how much you can surmise about the overall story.

Once you have done that, what I'd like you to note in the above piece is how this author has used a mix of formal and informal dialogue to convey how his characters speak. The narrator is obviously familiar with English and therefore uses contractions such as 'he's' and 'they'd', whereas Ephraim uses more stilted language, such as 'he is' and 'had not'.

Also note the use of the present tense in this segment. Present tense can be quite hard to sustain for an entire book, but it has been used very effectively by some authors. It lends a sense of immediacy to the narrative.

Writing exercise 3:

Try writing a story from your own life emulating how this story has been told.

Gathering Information

Most of your information, at least in the beginning, will come from your own memory. Below are some methods you can use to tap into those memories and then suggestions on where you can do some research in order to fill in any gaps.

Memory

Lists

This is a method most writing teachers will advocate, no matter what type of writing you intend to do. Making lists helps to trigger thoughts and also helps you to organise your ideas into coherent threads.

Researchers on memory recall say that writing one thought on a list can trigger others, and you will often find yourself summoning up a whole series of events via one simple item on a list. You might even find yourself remembering the events in vivid detail, as if they had happened yesterday.

While creative writers will often start with a single idea in the middle of a page and then jot down ideas triggered by that word in a fan around it, writers of non-fiction will most likely stick to linear lists, perhaps even numbered.

No one way is right or wrong; do whatever works for you.

The idea is to jot down your thoughts as they come to you, perhaps using major turning points in your life as the fulcrum. For instance, you might use the date of your marriage as one turning point, the dates of the birth of your children, the date you lost your parent or a sibling; any date that is significant in your life and is one you are unlikely to ever forget.

Examples of lists

- Marriage – meeting my husband, courtship, the big day, signs I ignored, honeymoon wakeup call
- Birth of first child – happiness tinged with sadness
- Birth of second child – building doom
- Divorce – enough is enough
- Rape – too painful to write about now
- Trip to USA – much needed escape, a shot at redemption
- Meeting counsellor – my saviour!
- Court case – building the case, problems we encountered, touch and go, would we win?
- Redemption – it's over! My new life

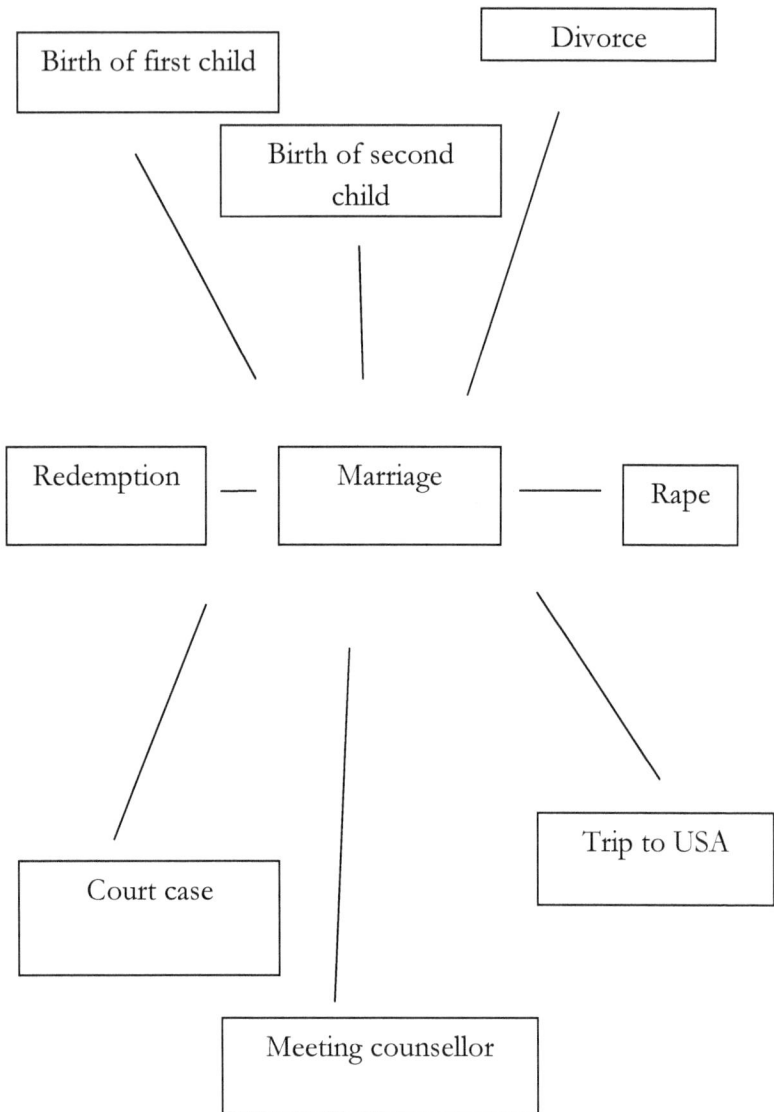

Birth of first child

Divorce

Birth of second child

Redemption — Marriage — Rape

Court case

Trip to USA

Meeting counsellor

If you're unsure how to go about making your list then one method is to take a large piece of paper, such as an A3 or bigger, and use a pencil or coloured crayons to jot down ideas as they come to you. Should you prefer making a virtual list then try using the online tool Scapple.

If you find any one memory resonates with you more than the others then go with that thread straight away and follow it until you feel it has reached its natural conclusion.

This might mean a lot of what you write will need to be discarded later, but you might be able to use it in subsequent stories, so I'd suggest you keep whatever you write.

Diaries and journals

If you've always kept a diary or journal, then you have a good base to use for your memoir. You should have accurate dates of when events occurred, details like the weather, how major current events had an impact on your life, and even how you felt at the time. It all depends on the detail included in your diary or journal.

Journals can form the basis of a really funny memoir, particularly if they were written when you were a child and had a distorted child's view of the world. Even tragic incidences could take on a humorous light.

I think here of Frank McCourt's *Angela's Ashes* and *'Tis*. Frank's portrayal of his life in *Angela's Ashes* is both tragic and funny. The neglect he suffered at the hands of his parents was awful. Yet he still manages to instil some sympathy in the reader for both his parents.

If you don't have a diary or journal, then there are other ways you can jog your memory.

Photographs

This is self-explanatory but is a really effective way of recalling events. If you already know what you want to write about, then try surrounding yourself with photos of that period in your life. By looking at photos of a particular time, you'll be able to recall who was there, what clothes you wore, your hairstyle, even what car was used to get you to the venue, or whether you went by train, bus, plane, or boat. Maybe even by cart, bicycle, roller skates/blade, or simply shank's pony.

Photos will also trigger memories of places as well as people, so they will help you to describe a beach house or a hotel, a campground, a mountain, a favourite picnic spot accurately.

You may have photographs of pets, farm animals or wild animals that have featured in your life. Often our animals are as much part of the family as the people.

Mementos

If you've done a lot of travelling you have no doubt collected mementos and paraphernalia on your various trips. Researchers have shown that touching an object can trigger clear memories of a time you're trying to bring to mind, so if you're trying to recall a particular episode, for example your visit to Africa in 1995, you might find it helps to surround yourself with the objects you bought while on that trip.

While doing this, close your eyes and touch the objects. Allow yourself to feel them, run your fingers over their shapes and imagine where you were when you bought them, perhaps what prompted you to make the purchase and what it was like at the time.

Try to identify how you felt then, whether it was hot or cold, whether it had been a happy or stressful day, what smells surrounded you.

This will help immerse you back into that frame of mind and should help jog long-buried memories just waiting to be retrieved.

If you find that these objects do trigger a memory or a feeling then start writing and go with that thread.

Meditation

If you don't have a journal or diary, and don't have any photos or mementos you feel are relevant to your story then you could try closing your eyes and travelling back to that time in your mind through meditation.

Meditation has been shown to enlarge the cerebral cortex, the area of your brain responsible for the most complex mental activities.

You might find that music from the period is really helpful in this process, though it might also prove to be distracting, and it's amazing what the mind will dredge up if given the chance.

Find somewhere that's quiet, where you can be alone and are unlikely to be disturbed, then close your eyes and focus on your breathing. You might find it helpful to imagine yourself descending a flight of ten steps. When you reach the final step, look around. What do you see?

If you're still not in the place you want to be then try taking a flight in your mind and skim over land, seas and mountain ranges until you reach the place in your memory. Imagine it in rich detail and when you emerge from your meditation write down what you saw, felt and thought.

Consult family and friends

I include this point with a certain amount of trepidation, as consulting other people about your memoir can be fraught with more problems than it's worth. However, this is your decision and if you feel you can negotiate the minefield that may come with asking other people for their impressions or memories of certain events then by all means do so.

People often have different primary senses, so while you might recollect the smells clearly, your brother might hark back to particular sights or sounds. This could add more colour and layers to your memoir.

However, please be aware that anyone you consult may wish for you to include their input in your memoir and you may offend them if you don't.

Other aids for memory recall

Research has shown that recalling events from your past can be aided in a number of ways.

Mood: Recalling memories is more efficient when the mood at the time the memory was laid down is replicated. I by no means want you do something that will make you really miserable when recalling unhappy or painful memories, but you might be able to aid the recall process if you play melancholy music when dealing with a gloomy period in your life.

Conversely, you could play uplifting music when trying to recall happy events, or simply smile or laugh, which will also elevate your mood.

Senses: Another proven path for recalling memories is to replicate the senses you felt at the time. So you could try to emulate the smells that were there; the feel of certain items; the taste of certain foods; the sounds you heard, perhaps via music or soundtracks of bird and animal calls; the sights you saw, via movies or documentaries or a trip back to the place you're writing about.

Physical exercise: While I'm certainly not advocating that you have to go on a fitness campaign before you write your memoir, research does indicate that a moderate level of exercise can help in the recall process by reducing stress and improving your alertness. So a brisk walk in the fresh air might reinvigorate a flagging memoir and help you recall more events from your past.

Mental exercise: Exercise is not only good for your body. Doing brain exercises such as puzzles, cross words and Sudoku, or one of the many brain training exercises available as apps these days, will improve your alertness and memory recall as well.

Diet: Eating a diet rich in antioxidants such as vitamins B, C and E, and Omega 3 fatty acids will also help with memory recall. Specifically they will assist your ability to recognise and retrieve memories. Antioxidants are found in fruit and vegetables, as well as in oily fish, such as salmon.

Rest: You will often find your memory will be better when you've had sufficient sleep, so you could try doing your memory recall directly after you wake or perhaps after a nap, or after you have emerged from a meditation.

Research

Up until now you have relied on your memory to recall events from your past, but what happens when your memory is no longer sufficient, or if you are writing about the effect an older person had on your life and you don't know much about their past?

This is where research comes in. As you will read later in more detail, periods of writer's block can be caused by a lack of knowledge that requires you to do some research.

How can that be? you might ask. You were there; you lived through it. Yes, I acknowledge that's true, but our memory is not always accurate and not always complete.

During your research, as you uncover paintings or photos from a particular time, you'll find these objects will trigger even more memories, which means research can work in conjunction with your memory.

So, you need to do some research. Where do you start?

Internet and search engines

These days the internet and search engines would be the first place to look. There are so many different sites and so many different search engines. I'll mention a few engines, such as Google, Bing, Yahoo, but there are many others.

If you need to research something about an older person who had an effect on your life, or who was in turn affected by someone in his or her past, then you could try sites like these:

- Ancestry.com and all its variations, such as Ancestry.co.uk, Ancestry.com.au and Ancestry.ca;

- The Church of Jesus Christ of Latter-Day Saints, who have a truly amazing resource for researching family history via their site familysearch.org;

- myheritage.com;

- usa.gov;

- recordclick.com;

- archives.gov;

- findmypast.com and its variations;

- genealogy.about.com;

- usgenweb.org;

- genesreunited.com.au;

- familytreemagazine.com.

Here again, there are so many different sites to choose from.

Simply type your question into the search engine bar and you will be given numerous options.

A word of warning is that sources on the internet can be inaccurate, so I would suggest you thoroughly research every source and check that the facts are correct. Follow a number of threads, not just one, and gradually the truth should emerge.

Despite the inaccuracies inherent in information gleaned from the net, it's still an excellent place to start and will often set you on the right path.

Local libraries

For many of us the local library will be our first port of call after we've completed our internet search. Local librarians are often extremely knowledgeable and very happy to help with enquiries, even hunting down information sources for you or suggesting where you might look next. Also, if you need to obtain a resource from either your state or national library, then this will often be delivered to your local library.

State, provincial or regional libraries

Another excellent resource for doing research is via your state, provincial or regional library. These are usually situated in the capital city of your region and so if you are a long way from the capital it might present a problem.

However, libraries are usually more amenable than archives to lending you material, even if you live in a rural area. The downside is that often these state libraries will only lend material to residents of that state, so if the research you're doing is in another state you might have difficulty borrowing it.

If you live in the same state, though, it's possible to have the state library send books to your local library for you to pick up. You will probably need to be a member of your state library and may also need to join your local library, if you haven't already. This depends on the rules of the state in which you live.

You can normally obtain items such as books, pamphlets, magazines, government publications, music scores, as well as CDs and DVDs.

Some items may not be available for borrowing but are available for reading at the state library venue. Examples of these are newspapers, reference sources, and any items deemed too fragile to lend out. There will be other restrictions so it's best to check with your state library.

Even though you can't borrow and take away restricted items, it's often possible to get copies of the originals. This would be subject to copyright laws.

National libraries

Most countries will also have a national library where copies of all publications from that country are held. Amongst the services offered, there is often an extensive family history research section where records are kept on microfilm and microfiche.

Many of these files are also available electronically and you may be able to access them remotely, though for others you may need to go into the library to do your research.

The National Library of Australia, for instance, offers links to various web sites where there is no charge to conduct research. Some of these offer global access, so you can even research family history in other countries, such as the UK. There are no fewer than 42 pages containing 414 links to free web sites.

Besides the links to free access sites, there are also links to licensed sites that require you to be a member of the national library in order to access them. I found 113 links on the National Library of Australia site and a further 191 links to material that can only be accessed at the library, provided you have a library card.

The downside of both these methods is that you need to live in Australia and supply an Australian address in order to obtain a card. Similar restrictions may apply in other countries, which could mean that access is limited to the country in which you live.

If you live in the USA, try the Library of Congress site for information. If you live in the UK or Canada try the British Library or the Library and Archives Canada. If you live in another country try typing 'family history (country name) free' into a search engine and see what you come up with. Anyone researching family history in India, for instance, will find a section listed under the British Library.

University libraries

If you have a university or universities near you, they will quite often allow community access to their libraries. You will of course need to register with them, but a quick online search of the universities closest to me revealed a vast array of family history research tools.

Special-interest libraries

Certain special-interest groups will have libraries of their own. One that comes immediately to mind is the American War Library, which houses information about all things military and about veterans who have fought in the conflicts in which the USA has been involved.

You will find libraries for classic cars and army libraries, so try thinking laterally on this one and type in various special-interest group names to see what you come up with. The results could be rewarding.

Historical societies

Most towns have a local historical society and these are a great place to glean information. If you're not sure how to contact them then try doing a web search or ask at your local library.

If you use a search engine to find the contact details for these societies, you will no doubt find links to other associations that you may not have thought about. In a quick search for a historical society in our area I found links to the history of wood-cutting and turning, a war museum, the history of the entire district, as well as links to famous people ranging from sculptors to benefactors.

A visit to the headquarters of these societies should put you in touch with people who are passionate about preserving local history and they should be able to provide you with valuable information.

Archives

When my sister and I were researching our family history a number of years ago, we often went to the archives that held the historical records for our province. As is the case with most archives, these were housed in the capital city, which happened to be relatively close to where we both lived, so if you're situated far from your capital city then this could pose a problem, as it's invaluable to be able to research the original documents.

The digital age has affected this type of research somewhat, but when we went to the archives the documents could not be taken out of the building so we had to take notebooks and jot down relevant information as we found it.

It's bit like a treasure hunt.

You may not have many clues to go on, maybe just a name, but as you continue to research you'll find various threads and will need to follow them.

You could compare it to unravelling a ball of yarn. Some of the threads you follow prove to be the wrong one and don't help to unravel the ball at all, but others are right and if you follow them logically, through all their twists and turns, you'll end up with a coherent picture of what really happened.

Searching archival records can be confusing. Sometimes it's like looking for the proverbial needle in the haystack, so it helps if you already have some information that can set you on the right track.

My sister and I found we had a number of false starts. There were many people who had the same name and were born or died at roughly the same time. Often all we had to go on was a birth or death date, so it took a lot of reading to at last find the right family.

None of this reading was wasted, though, as all the life stories were interesting and helped us to form a picture of what life was like for all people living during our relatives' lifetimes. This helped colour in the blanks as regards to social status and social norms. Some of the stories of people we read about have remained with me to this day.

Archival records are not indexed by a single name or under only one category, so you might have to sift through many different records from a number of different departments.

At your archives you should be able to find at least some or all of these:

Lists of immigrants
If you or your family were migrants then there will be a record of your entry into a country. These

migration records are usually kept at the national archives. A quick internet search turned up the National Archives of Australia, National Archives at New York City, National Archives (USA), and National Archives (UK), so if you do a search you will be able to find the site for your national archives.

Records of births, deaths, marriages, and divorces

The government of your state or region will have a registry of births, deaths, marriages, and divorces. Most will also have a section devoted to family history research. As these historical physical records are beginning to degrade, there is an increasing focus on transcribing and uploading this information in digital format, so you may find that the information you are after is already available in digital form.

Should you require copies or photographs, there is usually a charge involved.

Electoral rolls

Old electoral rolls can be found at the archives for your state, province, region or country.

If you would like to search for general information, such as who the Member of Parliament was for a certain area at a particular time and what political affiliation they had then this information is often online.

If you would like to search the actual current electoral rolls, you will need to visit the office where the roll is kept.

Wills and intestacies

Wills and intestacies can reveal volumes about a person. One of our relatives had owned seven houses and, although he had five children, he had left all seven houses to his youngest child, a girl. We were puzzled about this as it seemed unfair, but as we dug deeper, following the threads of letters written by the girl's siblings to the Master of the Supreme Court, begging not to be compelled to sell these houses, we discovered that this girl was in fact an epileptic, in the days before effective medication, and she had been left somewhat mentally incapacitated as a result. The rent from the houses provided her with an income. So our assumption about our great-grandfather had been totally incorrect. He was in fact a good and responsible man, doing his best to ensure his youngest child was provided for and would not become a financial burden on her siblings.

Records of inmates of insane asylums

Many local archives will contain records of who was admitted to insane asylums, psychiatric hospitals, prisons and correction centres. The national archives often contain records relating to the administration of these facilities, rather than details on the occupants. Depending on the archives concerned, you can also peruse diaries written by inmates. Many of these records are now available online, although you might have to pay a fee to access some of them.

Records of insolvencies

If one of your family was unable to pay a debt they may have declared bankruptcy or been declared insolvent, and there should be a record of that insolvency held at the national archives. Some insolvency records were held at various other departments, such as the Public Record Office, but the archives should be able to point you in the right direction.

Police gazettes

Police gazettes can sometimes be found in the archives or alternatively in state libraries, so you'll need to do a little detective work of your own to find out where they are kept in your region. In police gazettes you may find information about:

- criminals who have escaped from prison
- criminal activities, such as arson, assault, robbery and murder
- criminals discharged from prison
- people who are wanted by the police
- police appointments, promotions, and resignations
- reports on missing people
- soldiers or sailors who have deserted
- inquests

Results of inquests

The results of inquests and coronial reports are usually held at the state archives. Inquests are held when the identity of the deceased is unknown, when a homicide has occurred, when the cause of death is unclear, when the person died while in custody or while attempting to escape from custody, in cases of accidental or violent death, or if there has been a suicide.

Lists of people who were naturalised

Naturalisation occurs when a migrant to a country adopts the citizenship of their new country. Sometimes mass naturalisations were carried out. As the housing of these records varies from country to country, it's best to do an internet search to establish where your own particular naturalisation records are kept.

Lists of children enrolled at state or provincial schools

Depending on where you live and the laws applicable, you may be able to access lists of children who were enrolled in state-run schools. Besides admission registers, these records will also contain lists of who was given corporal punishment, details about school administration and applications for school buildings. Information about children admitted to orphanages, other institutions and about child migrants is usually kept in the state library rather than the archives.

Records of land tenure

If you need to know who owned a property at any particular time, most regions allow you to do a property title search. You may do the search yourself, provided you pay the prescribed fee, or you may have to pay an approved licensed searcher, such as a lawyer who specialises in conveyance and property title searches. Historic property ownership records are kept at the archives and you may be able to search some of these records without paying a fee. Check with both your state archives and your state library.

Maps

The archives contain a vast resource of maps of all types: geographical, topographical, survey, electoral, census, land tenure, etc.

Lists of public servants

If you had a relative who worked in the public service then there should be records available about their employment. As with all searches conducted at the archives, you might need to look under a number of different categories to find the information you need.

Telephone and street directories

Old post office directories can be found at the archives. These will often give you street maps as well, or you may be able to find old street directories in separate editions. The telephone directories will give you street addresses of your relatives and any other people you may be researching.

In these digital days, you may well be able to obtain scanned copies of original documents, but most archives I've dealt with require you to initiate your search in person at their premises, and while you might be able to make copies of certain information, you will not be allowed to remove any documents from the prescribed search room.

Most archives also provide a postal or online service where you can make certain enquiries. However, some years ago when I tried to make an enquiry about the Cape Town Castle online, I was told to use a paid researcher instead, so I'm not sure how successful this method would be. I guess it depends on the state or country you're dealing with and is certainly worth a try if you have to travel long distances to reach the archives yourself.

Bear in mind too that certain documents may be restricted and you may not be allowed access to them at all, or you may be required to apply for access to them. You will need to contact the archives closest to you to find out what type of access they will allow. This will no doubt vary from place to place and country to country.

Usually archives are strictly controlled and you are required to provide some form of identification, and you are restricted in what you can take into the building. This is to prevent damage to or theft of such valuable original documents.

Books and bibliographies

When I've been doing research for both fiction and non-fiction books, one of the best resources to find out information is to read books on the subject or books set in the time period you're dealing with. Here again, do an internet search for books on the subject you're interested in or contact your local, state, national or university library to see if they hold any books that could help you.

Besides the knowledge contained in the books themselves, I've often found lists for further reading by perusing the bibliographies at the backs of books on the subject. If you find something of interest, follow the thread and that thread might lead to further lists and yet more information.

Industry journals

If a member of your family was prominent in any type of industry then no doubt records of his or her achievements exist. A quick search turned up a whole host of magazines and journals on virtually every industry. At the very least, industry journals will provide you with valuable background information, even if not specific information about your relative.

Museums

When I needed to do research for my novel *Chameleon*, parts of which are taken from true-life family events, I found I needed to know a lot about my old home town as it had been in my parents' and grandparents' time. Much of what I was writing about occurred before I was even born, so I couldn't rely on memory to help me.

As I no longer lived in the town, or even in the same country by that time, my sister very kindly undertook a lot of the research for me. She received help from various sources but by far the most helpful source proved to be a lady who worked at the local museum, and who supplied her with photographs of the town as it had been during the periods mentioned in the book, as well as photographs of buildings, beaches and other places, such as the market square.

From these photographs I also managed to glean clothing fashion, the furniture that would have been in the houses, the farm implements, modes of transport and how these changed over time, as well as the makes of cars and carriages that were in vogue then. It was all incredibly useful and helped make the book far more authentic.

What I also found surprising is how intuitive the mind's eye can be, because much of what I had envisaged and already written as a proviso proved to be an accurate reflection of the reality.

Following on from the previous section under Archives on immigration records, we even managed to obtain a book from the museum which gave us

73

the names of the settlers who had arrived in the area from other countries, such as England and Prussia (this was before the days of German unification), and this proved to be an invaluable resource, as it listed spouses, number of children, ages, occupation, place of origin and the place where they settled.

You will find that there are specialist museums, such as those associated with war memorials, police, naval, aviation, farm machinery, and woodcutting museums etc, which will also be able to provide you with interesting information that will help to make your memoir more interesting, accurate and factual.

Local publications

Most districts have at least some publications put out by enthusiastic amateurs or by local historians. Check with your local historical society, farmers' association, women's guild and any relevant schools. These publications may be obtained directly from the organisation, school or society, or might be sold at local attractions, such as theme parks, cafes, national parks, wildlife parks, heritage parks, gift shops, and at natural features, such as famous waterfalls, rock formations, mountain ranges, rivers etc.

Genealogical societies

Researching family history is one of the most popular pastimes these days so you'll no doubt find a genealogical society in the capital city of your region, if not in your local area.

Genealogists are passionate about their work, and will be more than happy to help you with any queries you may have. You'll find they have vast libraries and a host of books you can buy.

Cemeteries

When I was a child my mother and aunt would often take my sisters and me down to our local cemetery to place flowers on the graves of dead relatives. This may seem macabre now, but as small children we actually enjoyed the experience. It was an opportunity to take a walk with our elders, as well as get to know about people we had never met. I can recall the sense of reverence we felt and also a strange connection.

Besides the stories that we learnt about our own relatives, we discovered some tragic facts about people buried in neighbouring graves too, and this fired our ever-active imaginations. I still to this day think of some of the gravestones in that cemetery. So, ghoulish as it sounds, cemeteries are a great place to find out about people who have passed on.

Unfortunately, a sad fact is that, for a variety of reasons, such as war, epidemics, poverty, or because there were no known living relatives, some people were buried in unmarked graves. Sometimes a number of bodies would be interred in the same grave.

However, there are records of some unmarked graves and who is buried in them. This is especially true of church burial grounds which may no longer be in use. Often someone, the local priest, or a caring amateur, may have recorded a plan of the burial sites and also recorded a list of names where individuals were buried.

The good news is that, as DNA techniques progress, many bodies that were buried in unmarked war graves are now being identified.

Cautions

While doing research, it may be tempting to follow a thread that is appealing rather than one that is factual. A case in point here might be if you have a desire to find nobility in your background, but instead the thread you are following indicates that you are in fact from a more lowly origin. You might even find that there are some undesirable aspects to the information you uncover, such as someone who was a murderer or committed some other terrible crime.

Keep in mind that the past can't be changed and that you're not responsible for what other members of your family did. If you would rather not disclose something about your relatives then that's fine – not everything has to be made public – but there's also no point in deluding yourself that things weren't as they were.

However, whether your findings are good or bad, it's still worth checking the information with a number of sources to make sure it's right.

One member of our family is a keen genealogist but unfortunately he isn't all that good at getting the facts right, so important information such as birth dates are recorded incorrectly and this could cause problems for our descendants if they have only his records to go on.

Be particularly sceptical about information gleaned from the internet. While the internet is a valuable resource and rightly the first place you would search these days, it's still advisable to check a number of different sources before believing that you have the true facts.

When my sister and I were researching our family history at the archives, we found that we followed many leads that proved to be incorrect.

When you're presented with a number, for instance, and seem to have hit a dead end or perhaps arrived at a destination that doesn't seem to be right, maybe try looking at that number from a different angle. When it comes to addresses, the numbers 3a/27 might refer to the lot number or to the unit and street number.

A number such as 19 18 may refer to the reference number of an entry rather than the date 1918.

Having detailed all the ways in which you can do research, I'll now finish by telling you not to waste too much time on this necessary and often enjoyable part of writing a memoir.

If you feel you don't know enough about your subject to even get started then by all means do the research required – just don't make the very common mistake of devoting so much time to it that you never get round to writing your memoir. Researching can become addictive and it's easy to waste time and procrastinate rather than getting on with the nitty-gritty of the story you want to tell.

Also, don't be tempted to include everything that you've learnt during your research in your memoir. As with any good storytelling, you need to include only that which is relevant to the story you're writing at that moment. If some of your other research interests you, you could write another memoir about that, or simply keep it in separate files where others can access it if they wish to. If it does have some bearing on your story but isn't immediately relevant, then you could consider adding this as endnotes at the back of your book, but I wouldn't recommend it.

It would be as well to note too that, while I have given you an extensive list of where you can do research should you need to, please don't make the mistake of confusing memoir with family history. By all means write a family history if that's the way your research guides you, but if you want to stick to writing a memoir then the only part of your research that is relevant is that which has a bearing on the relationship you had with someone in your past.

So if your grandmother had an amazing influence on your life and your story is about your relationship, then you will no doubt need to research her life and what influenced her in order to fully understand her. You might even need to research her parents in order to understand what shaped her and her philosophy, but make sure you keep on track and write about how what you learnt from your grandmother helped shape your life.

Conclusion

A tip provided by the Queensland State Archive site suggests that you make sure you record all your research findings, such as the site where you found the information etc, so that you can go back and check it or follow different leads should you need to.

Summary

When writing memoir you can gather information in a number of different ways:

Memory

- Make lists
- Consult diaries or journals
- Look at photographs
- Turn to mementos
- Meditate
- Consult family and friends
- Try other aids for memory recall

Research

- Use the internet and search engines
- Visit local libraries
- Visit state or regional libraries
- Visit your national library
- Visit university libraries
- Search out special-interest libraries
- Contact historical societies
- Visit the archives where you will find:
    - Lists of immigrants
    - Records of births, deaths, marriages, and divorces
    - Electoral rolls
    - Wills and intestacies
    - Records of inmates of insane asylums

- Records of insolvencies
- Police gazettes
- Results of inquests
- Lists of people who were naturalised
- Lists of children enrolled at state or provincial schools
- Records of land tenure
- Maps of all types (geographical, topographical, survey, electoral, census, farms etc)
- Lists of people employed in the public service.
- Telephone and street directories

- Read books and peruse bibliographies
- Consult industry journals
- Visit museums
- Obtain local publications
- Contact genealogical societies
- Visit cemeteries

Writing exercise 1:

Write at least half a page on 'I remember how ...'

Writing exercise 2:

Read the following excerpt:

But we didn't see Bert all that week and had despaired of saving the bay when he arrived at our side over the weekend, pulling to a halt in dramatic fashion, setting the bay back on his skinny heels. Bert and the bay had lost weight. Bert's brown, bird-like eyes glittered almost feverishly beneath thick black brows. His face was paler, his cheeks sunken above his rough black beard. He was wearing a pair of dirty blue overalls and I wondered, from the stains, whether they'd ever been washed. The bay's thin flanks were hollow, his ribs showed starkly beneath the saddle and the sore on his withers was raw and open, blood seeping into the leather of the saddle.

'Oh, Bert, you shouldn't be riding him like that,' I blurted, unable to contain my anguish as Bert and the bay fell into step beside us.

Bert frowned, but quickly masked his anger with a smile. He ignored my remark.

'How's youse, then? I've been working so hard, man. Old man's had me cutting hay. Such hard work, man.' He was clearly trying to impress.

We weren't.

'Would you like to sell your horse?' I asked, tactlessly.

The horses' hooves thudded on the dirt track of the firebreak.

A flicker of annoyance passed over Bert's face. Shane snorted, tossed his mane, and snaked his head towards the bay, which was walking too close.

'No, man. I need him to work. And what have youse been doing all week, hey?' he continued, trying to charm.

'But he's sick, Bert. He needs care.' I glanced at the bay, my eyes drawn to the red patch on the saddle.

'I's been working so hard, man. No time for play. Not like youse girls, hey?' Bert pretended not to hear.

'We'd like to buy him,' I stated baldly, not giving up.

Bert went silent, summing up the situation. The horses' heads bobbed in unison as we plodded along the firebreak.

A cunning look came into Bert's eyes as he turned to look at me.

'Okay, man. Twenty.'

'But he's so thin, Bert. We haven't got twenty.'

'He's sick,' added Yvette.

Bert watched me carefully through hooded eyes, his thoughts transparent on his thin face. If he reduced the price, would he stand a chance with me? He obviously thought 'yes'.

'Okay, man, eighteen.'

I did a quick mental calculation. That would take all I had, but we had food in the house, should be able to survive until my mom came home.

'Okay, Bert. That's great. Can we take him today?'

Bert looked sulky. It had dawned on him that his plan had backfired. Once we had the bay, we were unlikely to see him again.

'No, man. I've got work to do today. Youse can come for him tomorrow. Bring the money then. Youse had better come back with me now, though, so youse know how to find the farm. Come meet my old man.' Bert had brightened up again, clearly hoping to impress us – the wealthy landowner, hardworking man of the land.

We followed him along the main road with buses whizzing past in a whoosh of hot air. Africans wolf-whistled and shouted remarks from the windows as the buses hurtled past. The sun was hot on our backs, burning our shoulders.

Bert led the way down a winding dirt road leading to a squat, ugly house crouching amongst long grass and stunted trees. Grey, rough pole fences signalled a cattle yard where an elderly, grey-haired man in a dirty white vest with grey suspendered trousers was inspecting some red Afrikaner cattle. Two black men brandished sticks at the beasts.

'*Pa*,' Bert's tone was deferential. The bombast was gone. He spoke quickly to the old man, their voices low, so we couldn't overhear.

The old man squinted at us through half-closed eyes, taking in Shane and Whiskey and, lastly, our two forms. His eyes lingered on us for a long time. I squirmed uncomfortably, feeling dirty under his gaze, stripped naked, exposed.

He spoke again to Bert, and then turned back to the cattle, dismissing us with his attitude.

'My pa says it's okay. You can take him tomorrow. But he wants twenty.'

My heart sank.

'We haven't got twenty.'

Yvette looked at me regretfully. We had come so close. Disappointed, we took a last look at the bay, standing now with his head hanging, one gaunt hind leg resting, ears out sideways. We turned Shane and Whiskey and made our way back up the dirt road, waving goodbye to Bert as we went.

Did you enjoy this piece?

If yes, then what did you enjoy about it?

If no, then what didn't you enjoy about it?

Write down what you can glean from this piece, such as who are the characters, how old are they, what are their social circumstances, what are they like, what are their likes and dislikes, what emotions do they feel, what is the relationship between the characters, what do you think might be happening, and where is this piece set? Go into plenty of detail and see how much you can surmise about the overall story.

Once you have done that, what I'd like you to note in the above piece is how this author has given detailed descriptions of setting and characters. She has also anchored the scene at various points by reminding us where they are and what they're doing.

Writing exercise 3:
Try writing a story from your own life emulating how this story has been told.

Getting Started

So you have your memories, you may even have written short pieces, anecdotes or even whole chapters, and you've done all the research you need to start. Where to now?

Who is the story for?

The first thing you need to decide is who is this story for. Is it for yourself, or for your family and friends, or is it intended for publication and perhaps a global audience?

If the story is intended only for you then you have no restrictions on what you include. You don't have to worry about who you might hurt or what you say. You also don't have to worry about the accuracy of your observations, as no one can dispute what you think or feel. The one reservation would be that if you include too many home truths then you may want to ensure no one ever has access to your memoir, even after your death, unless you want to leave a parting-shot legacy and therefore a sour taste in the minds of those left behind.

You may simply want to record events so that you don't forget them, or so that you can relive a certain time in your life. You may have had a particularly happy or traumatic period that you experienced and writing it down will immortalise it in your mind.

If the record is for your family and friends then don't be tempted to allow too many people to have input into what you record. We all have differing memories and you may find yourself bogged down and unable to write if you try to please everyone. Remember: this is your memoir and it's a record of how you recollect things. A brief disclaimer near the beginning of the book to this effect should clear up any controversy, although this can't be guaranteed, as discussed earlier.

If you intend for your work to be published, whether it be via traditional publishing or self-publishing, then you need to pay more attention to issues such as libel and defamation. If you intend to air dirty linen then make sure that you have sound advice so you don't find yourself embroiled in legal battles.

None of these above paths is correct or incorrect; it's up to you which route you take.

Point of View

There are three points of view we can use to write our memoir and these are expressed as first, second and third person.

First person

Example: I/we picked up my/our grandfather's letter.

First person is the most obvious choice to use when writing a memoir. The story is about you and your thoughts and feelings, so it makes sense to write using first person, in this case the singular version of first person, which is 'I'.

Using first person has a number of advantages, not least of which is that it feels more intimate and will draw your reader into your story more. It will also feel more authentic to your family and friends.

A downside is that you must then stick to only your point of view, that is, you can't give someone else's viewpoint, as you could if you were writing in third person, which is commonly used in fiction.

This isn't a major problem, though, because you can still write down what you interpreted another's feelings or thoughts to be from their facial expression or body language. Your interpretation may be incorrect, of course, but that only serves to heighten any tension and suspense in your story so it's not a bad thing.

Second person

Example: You picked up your grandfather's letter.

Second person is seldom used for full-length works, although it is sometimes used in short stories.

I actually enjoy writing in second person. I find it liberating, but not many people enjoy it and judges of competitions and buyers for magazines often avoid it so I wouldn't recommend you use this, especially not for writing your memoir.

Third person

Example: He/she/they picked up his, her, their grandfather's letter.

Third person is very common in fiction and I have known some people who have written their memoirs in third person, but I wouldn't recommend it unless you're writing your memoir as fiction. You lose the advantages of writing in first person, the intimacy and immediacy, and still don't really overcome any disadvantages.

If you do decide to fictionalise your memoir and want to use third person, then you'll most probably write it in third person limited, which is as close to first person as you can get while still writing in third person.

Remember, give only one character's point of view per scene or per chapter, otherwise you risk alienating your reader. You can see more about this important point in my book *Self-Editing Your Novel.*

What voice should you adopt?

The path you choose will, however, affect what you write and how you write it, because we all tend to speak and write with many voices. We don't, for instance, speak to a child in the same way we speak to an adult. We use appropriate language and may even alter the tone of our voice.

So if you're writing for yourself alone, then you will most likely vent your feelings freely, being entirely honest with yourself.

If you're writing for family and friends, you may temper what you write to some extent and focus instead on aspects that are likely to be of interest to them.

If you're writing for publication, you will need to make sure the story is told in an entertaining way, using all the story-telling principles of pace, suspense, action etc that apply to writing fiction, while keeping your story real. More on this aspect later.

The cast

Once you've decided who you're writing for, which will affect both the tone and the content of what you write, you also need to decide who will feature in your memoir.

This may sound obvious. It's your memoir, so you are obviously the star of the story, and the rest of the cast are all your family and friends and anyone who has crossed your path.

If you're writing for yourself, or for your family and friends, then that's fine; you have your cast already. However, if you would like to publish your work for general consumption then you might need to focus on only some of the people who have featured in your life rather than on everyone.

Every good story needs a protagonist (good guy) and an antagonist (bad guy), so your **main cast** would have at least two characters in it, but you might need more to tell the story you would like to tell. Many writing teachers advocate a main cast of between two and five.

Besides the main cast, all good stories have a **supporting cast** as well.

While some authors manage to get away with large casts, generally speaking readers find large casts confusing, so your memoir will work better if you stick to maybe only two to five main characters and five to ten supporting characters, otherwise it becomes hard for readers to keep track of who is who.

This principle of limiting your cast often doesn't sit well with memoirists, because they feel anyone left out may be offended. That may be the case, and please remember, as I've said before, these are not hard and fast rules; there are no rules when it comes to writing. This is your memoir and you must write it as you see fit, but, and it's a big 'but', if you intend for your memoir to be traditionally published, then sticking to these storytelling principles will help to achieve that.

So you might choose to have yourself, your grandmother, your father and your elder brother as your main cast, and then your mother, your grandfather, an uncle and two family friends as your supporting cast. Your cast is up to you and can be as large or as small as you choose.

Cast and theme

To help you decide who should feature, if you haven't done so already, now is the time to decide on the focus of your memoir. Is this about your young life when you learnt some important life lessons? If it is, then who was most instrumental in teaching you those lessons, and who was most in the way of you achieving those goals?

It's unlikely that your whole family will have had equal influence over you, so perhaps your father was the one who stood in the way of you achieving your goals and your elder brother was the most instrumental in showing you how to achieve them in spite of your father's bad example.

The main thing is to focus on the point of your story or the theme, and include only those bits of your life that help to illustrate that theme.

Identifying a theme

Choosing a theme can present problems and there's no quick answer to help you identify the theme in your work, but here are some examples that might help you decide.

Let's take a couple of different scenarios and then see how their themes might shape up.

Scenario 1

- Earliest memory of my dad carrying me on his shoulders
- My brother being born
- Mom's illness
- Dad teaches us to march in the garden
- Getting Spike, my first dog
- Going to school
- Moving house
- Dad teaches us weapons' skills

- Dad creates a scene in the park
- My brother dies
- I find Dad crying
- Uncle Luke visits
- Holiday at the beach
- Dad marches in the parade
- Dad in hospital

If we look at this list, Dad features quite prominently, no fewer than seven times, so already a theme is beginning to emerge. If we examine the other points on the list where Dad is not mentioned, we realise that he may well have been there or had a strong impact on those events anyway. For instance, where was he during the birth of your brother? How did he react? How did he behave during your mom's illness? Was he supportive or did he fall apart? And how did he cope with the death of your brother?

Let's make some assumptions and come up with what may be the story of your fictional life. Let's assume that your dad fought in World War II and received medals for the part he played in a famous battle, but that secretly he always felt he could have done better, that he was afraid and undeserving. So many good men died and he couldn't save them.

His war-time experiences and his feelings of inadequacy translated into a fanatical need to teach you and your brother how to march and learn weapons' skills, which resulted in the tragic death of your brother. Eventually your dad learnt to forgive himself for both your brother's death, and for his inability to save his fellow soldiers, and, shortly before his death, he takes part in a military parade with pride.

So the theme for this memoir could well be how your father's World War II war-time experiences had a profound impact on your life. Your higher theme could be the necessity to forgive oneself, to come to terms with the past.

Examining the list again, we can see that some items on the list don't appear to belong, such as Mom's illness, getting Spike, going to school, moving house, Uncle Luke's visit and the holiday at the beach, so it would be best to leave these out unless they have a direct bearing on the story you have decided to tell.

To extrapolate further, if your dad's reaction to your mom's illness was intense and had a direct influence on how he subsequently behaved, then leave it in. If your dad's one act of kindness to you was giving you Spike, then that should be included as well. Uncle Luke's visit might have had a profound effect on your dad and enabled him to forgive himself for what happened to your brother and during the war. Only those points that help to illustrate your theme or have a direct bearing on it should be included.

You will note too that although this memoir is about you and the effect your father's war-time experiences had on you, you will no doubt need to do plenty of research into your father's life and his war-time career in order to understand him fully.

Scenario 2

- Marriage

- Moving to the farm
- Birth of first child
- Birth of second child
- Holiday down south
- Storm wipes out crops
- Floods!
- Drought
- Learning to milk cows
- Helping a cow give birth
- Learning to drive a tractor
- Tractor accident
- Cows on the main road
- Trip to capital city
- Trip overseas
- Neighbours attacked and murdered
- Migrate to new country

Looking at this list it's obvious that the farm and farming play a big role in your made-up life story, featuring no fewer than ten times.

The fictional story behind this scenario could be that city-slicker you marries a man who farms in a third-world country, and together you suffer through all the vagaries of weather, low commodity prices, political upheavals, anything that has an influence on how you manage to farm. However, when your good friends and neighbours are brutally attacked and murdered in their home, you weigh up the costs to your family and decide to migrate to a make a fresh start in a new country.

So the theme of this memoir could be the joys and hardships of farm life. Your higher theme could be adaptability, or how humans can adapt to almost any situation.

Again, certain points on your list don't seem to fit in with this theme, so you could eliminate things like holiday down south, trip to the capital city and trip overseas, unless these have a direct bearing on the story you want to tell. So, if your trip overseas made you realise there was another way to live and make a living apart from farming where you have been, you could leave that in, as long as you don't include too much detail about the trip and allow it to become a travelogue.

This scenario could also lead to a sequel: your fresh start in your new country.

Summary

- Who is this story for?
  - Yourself?
  - Your family and friends?
  - Publication and a global audience?
- What point of view should I use?
- What voice should I adopt?
- Who is my main cast?
- Who is my supporting cast?
- What is the theme of my memoir?
- Who helped shape that theme?

Writing exercise 1:

Write at least half a page on 'The funniest thing that happened to me ...'

Writing exercise 2:

Read the following excerpt:

'Jus, man. Look at these shoes.' I waggled my feet back and forth to draw Shirley's attention.

'What's wrong with them?' Shirley said, eyes fixed on my waving feet.

'They're black and they're huge.'

'Oh.' Shirley took a bite of her sandwich. The sulphurous smell of boiled egg drifted to me. 'They're not so bad. They're new.'

'They might be new, but they're ugly.'

'They're not so ugly. Better than your last pair.'

I sat up straighter. 'You didn't like my last pair?' I'd only worn the darn things for over a year and she'd never said anything. Not that my mum would have bought me new ones earlier, anyway. It had taken me ages to get her to agree to buy these.

'These are better.'

'But they make my feet look *huge*!'

Shirley stopped mid-chew and turned solemn eyes on me. 'They don't make your feet *look* big, Peggy. Your feet just *are* big.'

Did you enjoy this piece?

If yes, then what did you enjoy about it?

If no, then what didn't you enjoy about it?

Write down what you can glean from this piece, such as who are the characters, how old are they, what are their social circumstances, what are they like, what are their likes and dislikes, what emotions do they feel, what is the relationship between the characters, what do you think might be happening, and where is this piece set? Go into plenty of detail and see how much you can surmise about the overall story.

Once you have done that, what I'd like you to note in the above piece is how this author has used almost all dialogue to illustrate a point she is trying

107

to make. She hasn't set the scene or anchored it at any point. She has also used timing to deliver the humour in her piece.

Writing exercise 3:

Try writing a story from your own life emulating how this story has been told. Once you have done that you could try rewriting that same scene this time adding a setting and anchoring it at various points during the story. Try to keep the timing and humour intact, though. Don't allow the setting or anchoring to detract from the comic timing.

The Nuts and Bolts

So, you've decided who your memoir is going to be for, who is going to feature most prominently in it, and what your memoir is going to be about, that is, the theme. Now how do you go about actually writing it?

Character files

This doesn't work for everyone, but if you're an organised person you might like to follow some of the principles of fiction writing, whereby you make a file for each of your characters.

You can do this in a number of ways: as a computer file, in an actual physical folder or file, or on index cards. Many books on writing also contain lists of character traits which you can photocopy and then fill in. These are likely to be more detailed than you will need for people you know, as you will already have details such as hair and eye colour embedded in your memory, but if you're changing a character to avoid liability, or to avoid hurting someone's feelings, or if you've decided to fictionalise your memoir, then this method might work well for you.

Another method that might help you to keep your characters separate and distinct is to allocate a different file colour to each.

Writing for traditional publication

If you've decided to write in order to be traditionally published then the next piece of advice applies to you.

Most traditional publishers want books that are between 80,000 and 100,000 words, ideally 90,000 words. This would mean that you need to write roughly 30 chapters which are each 3,000 words long. I know this sounds prescriptive, and of course you've no need to stick to this advice slavishly. This just gives you an idea what a traditional publisher would be looking for.

So how do you achieve this?

Firstly, go back to the list you made near the beginning of this book. Have you identified a theme? Circle all those points which tie in with that theme and see if you can arrange them into what you feel will form a cohesive story.

Another important tip that applies to those who would like their book to be traditionally published is to see if you can identify a secondary or higher level theme as well. So while your memoir may be about your treatment at the hands of a mentally ill mother, your other more altruistic reason for writing this memoir is to show that it is possible to be happy in even the most adverse conditions. It's this higher theme, or added layer to your memoir that is often the key to achieving publishing success.

Once you have decided on all the above matters, if you can, write roughly 3000 words on each topic. When finished, these will make up your 90,000-word memoir.

Writing for other reasons

The above advice is very valid for anyone writing a memoir intended for traditional publication. However, what if you have no intention of going down that route?

Well, the good news is that anything goes. It's your story and you can write it and tell it any way you choose. In fact, if you're intending to self-publish or indie publish, research carried out by Mark Coker of Smashwords has shown that when it comes to ebooks, longer books (over 150,000 words) actually sell better. The same would not apply to the print versions of those books, though, and this is because large or thick books are heavier and therefore cost more to print, buy and post. They can also look intimidating to the reader, who might instead choose a thinner book to read.

Print issues aside, though, your memoir could be as little as 1,000 words or as long as 200,000 words. It really is up to you how much you'd like to tell and how you would like to tell it.

The writing process

There are two main methods you can use for writing your memoir: random or planned. As mentioned earlier, whichever method you prefer, it might still be worthwhile to go back to your initial list and see if you can identify a theme. If you can identify a theme, circle all those points that tie in with your theme and then see if you can arrange them into what you feel will form a cohesive story.

Random

If you have managed to identify a theme and circled all those points which fit in with that theme then you can begin to write in what I call the 'random' method. So, if you find that any one memory resonates with you more than the others then go with that thread and follow it until you feel it has reached its natural conclusion.

Something to be aware of as you write is that the writing process can trigger memories and emotions that are extremely painful. You might find yourself crying or angry, and the feelings can be really overwhelming. Be prepared for this and follow the feelings as much as you can, because it's the feelings any piece of writing evokes that most people want to experience as they read.

This process could take minutes, hours, days, weeks, or months.

So what do you do if you can't identify a theme no matter how hard you try? Well, if this is you, don't worry; a theme might emerge as you write. (Some people find it very hard if not impossible to ever identify a theme.) If you haven't managed to decide on a theme then pick any of the items on your list and just follow the same process mentioned above.

Once you have followed these threads and written down stories following your feelings, you might find you end up with a random mix of seemingly unconnected anecdotes, so what do you do next?

The answer is to try to find a common thread amongst them. In other words: at this stage, look for a theme. If you do identify a theme then this might mean that a lot of what you've written will need to be discarded from your present memoir, but you might be able to use it at a later date in subsequent stories, so I'd suggest that you keep whatever you've written.

A word of caution here.

If you decide to write in a random method and your anecdotes or chapters are written out of sequence, just make sure that when you go over your completed and assembled work you haven't repeated yourself or explained the relationship between people in Chapter 20 when you should really have explained this relationship in Chapter one.

Planned

If the random method doesn't sound like you then you could try planning instead. In practice, this might not save you a lot of time or writing but it could. So, how do you plan?

Going back to your list, examine it carefully and see if you can identify a theme.

If you have found a theme then circle those points on your list that tie in with that theme and see if you can arrange them into what you feel would make a good story. Once these are arranged then write about each item in a linear way, for instance from 1971 all the way through to 2001, starting with the first point on your newly arranged list and continuing until you reach the end of your book.

Short stories

If you would rather not write your memoir as one long document, there is a third method you could try, namely writing your memoir as a series of short stories. It would probably work best if each story had a similar theme, but this is not essential if the memoir is just for you and your family. You could devote one story to each incident you'd like to record, and the collection could encompass a variety of topics, such as the funny anecdote about your visit to the beach with Uncle George, and then the sad tale of how your faithful family dog Springer was killed by a snake. This method lends itself to writing using the random method, but be aware that you'll need to assemble your final collection of stories carefully so they fit together well.

How do I make my memoir interesting?

I am often asked: how can I write my memoir so that anyone will want to read it?

Underlying this question, of course, is the fear we will bore people, that we'll leave a negative rather than a positive legacy – and that's the last thing most of us want to do.

My answer to this is that most people who have a connection with you will find what you have to say interesting, regardless of how it is written, but if you would like to ensure it's as entertaining as possible then my advice is to write your memoir how you would speak, as if you were having a conversation with your family and friends, rather than from a remote and formal point of view.

If it helps, focus on one person and 'tell' them the story as you would if you had them next to you. Picture them listening as you recount your tale and if you sense they would find something boring then maybe leave that part out. If you find yourself picturing a child as you write, be careful that you don't adopt a patronising tone or 'talk down' to anyone.

Another excellent way to keep people entertained is to vary the stories, so mix in some funny anecdotes with some perhaps tragic or sad ones, some interesting facts with some frivolous ones.

If you would like to include details such as your date of birth, which school you attended and what work you did and where and when, then by all means do so, but don't feel that these have to be in the body of your memoir. If you feel that the information is a tad dry for the story you're trying to tell but still want to include it somewhere in your book then try, for instance, having a family tree at the back or front of the book. You could even highlight the names of the people you mention in your memoir if you so choose, but this isn't essential.

Other facts like the name of the school you attended and the dates you attended it could be included at the back of the book. This way, if anyone would like to know this information there will be a record of it in a convenient place, but you won't be boring anyone by including it in your story.

Follow the emotion

Good stories often succeed because they make the reader feel some sort of emotion while reading. They really empathise with the characters and want them to either succeed or fail, to achieve their goals or fall flat on their face.

With this in mind, as you write your memoir, write about what you recall passionately. It's the emotions that come through and that you instil in others through your writing that will make people want to read your memoir.

Remember, you don't have to write in sequence, so if one section of your memoir grabs you more than another then start there and follow the passion.

Write passionately about what you do recollect and leave out what you don't.

Allow yourself to sink into the scene. Imagine the sights, sounds, smells, tastes, textures. This is where your collection of objects comes in. Touch them, smell them, allow the senses to take over.

Follow the emotion because that is what people want to experience as they read.

Storytelling principles

Overall structure

When telling your story, there are a few principles about the structure of storytelling that could apply if you would like your memoir to be as interesting and readable as it can be.

Assuming you're going to write a standard 30-chapter memoir, the initial guideline is that the first third of your book should be used to introduce your main characters. By this I mean the main characters you've chosen for this particular story. You could also raise some pertinent questions, such as 'what is the real reason behind Uncle Percy's disappearance?' in the reader's mind, and pose some problems that your characters need to solve.

The second third of your story should contain all the action and interaction between those main characters and your supporting cast of more minor characters. All the questions that form the heart of any good story should be introduced during this section and any problems your main characters face are also included.

During the final third of your story you won't raise any more questions and you'll start to answer some of the questions raised in the first two thirds of your memoir.

As with any good yarn, your memoir also needs a climax and a resolution.

The climax would be when there is a major turning point in your life, for instance when you finally have a showdown with your alcoholic father.

The resolution would take place during the final chapter or final two chapters of your memoir.

Components of storytelling

Create a hook

A 'hook' is a word, sentence, phrase or paragraph that immediately draws your reader into the story. This is particularly important at the start of your memoir in your very first scene, but it won't do any harm to examine each scene to see if you can start it in a better way. Don't overdo this or allow it to interrupt the flow of your story or it could become annoying.

Set the scene

This is often called 'orienting' a scene, or telling the reader where the action is taking place.

Soon after the start of your scene, ensure that you include a brief description of the setting, so if it's at an old house, you could begin by describing the way the light filters through the dirty windows, the way the dappled shadows from trees outside fall on the floorboards. This often needs only one or two lines but straight away informs the reader where your characters are at that time and can also set the tone or mood. If you can, incorporate some sort of action and a 'hook' into this brief description of setting.

While your characters will then go on to do something even more interesting and speak about interesting things, you do need to throw in small clues at convenient places to remind your reader where this scene is happening. These small clues are called 'anchoring'. More about anchoring scenes later.

Have plenty of action in the scene

The key to any good story is to keep the pace moving. If you think about it, which would draw your attention more: a person running down the street or someone sitting on a park bench? Clearly it would be the person who is actually doing something. You would immediately wonder about the person who is running. Who or what is he running from, where is he running to and why?

The action doesn't have to be violent. It can even be subtle, but the point is that action is more interesting than inaction, so make your characters do something, even if it's only to stand up and pour a cup of tea.

Use all five senses

Most good writers will do this automatically, as it's part of the 'show don't tell' advice we are so often given, but it doesn't do any harm to check that you have done this correctly. A quick run through each page to make sure you have at least one of the senses per page will help your memoir to come to life. While you're at it, make sure you don't use only one sense over and over again too.

For instance, if your hearing is not good, you may have omitted sound from your memoir.

Dialogue

This won't always apply, but, generally, as soon as someone is talking your reader will find it more interesting. This also gives you the opportunity to show more about the people in your memoir by revealing their attitudes and beliefs.

Body language and gestures

This could just as easily be included under the heading of dialogue because body language can reveal volumes as well. Much of our communication is non-verbal. Some scientists claim that non-verbal communication is as high as 93 per cent, but most agree it can be as high as 60 or 70 per cent. Whatever the case, this is still a significant figure and as writers we can't afford to ignore this important part of our communication.

Allowing a reader to intuit what characters are thinking or feeling by interpreting their body language and gestures is a powerful way to make your characters more real to your reader.

If your reader is able to interpret clues about what the characters really feel rather than what they portray to the world, you will engage your readers more and they won't be able to put your memoir down. Readers love to identify with the feelings of your characters, so allow them to interpret the story in their own way.

Combine some of the elements

Making your words work harder by having them fulfil a number of functions can only improve your writing.

So, you could use a sentence containing body language to also convey information about the setting, particularly when you're trying to anchor a scene. For example:

Lillian looked back in silence as the trading store slowly receded into the distance — the only home she had ever known — squatting sullenly on the landscape under a lone eucalypt, surrounded by a horde of dusty urchins who shouted and waved as the cart ground its way along the dirt road towards Umtata.

From this sentence, we know Lillian is feeling melancholy because she is leaving her one and only home. We also know the trading store is not particularly attractive and it's in a fairly bleak or barren rural setting. The children she's leaving behind are not hers or related to her. They're poor but happy and kindly disposed towards her. We also know this story must be set in a period when carts were used as transport and that the cart is moving slowly. So, in one sentence, we have mood, setting, sound, and action. The words are working really hard.

How about this one?

Mom turned at the lights and went past Frere hospital, negotiating her way through the myriads of buses on their way to Mdantzane, the black township on the outskirts of East London.

The lady at the SPCA wasn't pleased to see us.

'Jus, man, it's late. Youse is lucky I'm still here. Normally shut the gate at five,' she said. 'But okay, man, youse might as well come in. But make it quick, hey?'

Mom smiled apologetically and we made our way past the howling, excited dogs to where Buster sat, quiet and obedient, wondering what all the fuss was about – until he saw us, then his body erupted into a frenzy of crazed wriggles as he wagged his stumpy tail for all it was worth.

We patted him and crooned over him and tried to assuage the guilt we felt at leaving him in the kennel. With heavy hearts, we said goodbye, shutting the kennel gate while we held him inside, watching the disappointment and sadness creep back into his eyes.

Jet was sitting sedately in her run, ignoring the cats on either side of her. She came forward happily, mewing softly as I stroked her head and cuddled her in my arms, but turned *away disdainfully when I placed her on the floor and left the cage.*

'The cat's not eating, man. Doesn't like anything I give her,' the lady confided.

Mom looked stricken.

From this we know Mom and the author are in a car and it's dusk or at least dark enough to turn the lights on. We know they're in a town and it's probably in a poor area, probably somewhere in Africa. The lady who runs the SPCA is poorly educated and has a grudging manner. Mom is feeling diffident about worrying anyone but is nevertheless determined to see the dog and cat that have been reluctantly housed in the kennels. Buster the dog is delighted to see them, while Jet the cat is pleased at first but then is standoffish. It's heartbreaking for them to leave both pets behind again. Mom, in particular, feels the separation acutely. Both Mom and the author are animal lovers.

As you can see, we can infer a lot even from a short passage.

Anchor the scene at strategic points

This point could come under 'setting the scene', but it is a slightly different concept to 'orienting' a scene.

By anchoring, I mean strategically seeding sentences, clauses and phrases throughout a scene to remind the reader where the action is taking place. As mentioned before, if you can combine these with other elements, such as the senses, action, body language and gestures, your words are working harder and your writing will be more appealing.

Examples of anchoring are:

'What it is?' Catherine's voice echoed off the cave walls.

And later:

Mandla stood a while, looking first from Catherine then to Eunice then out over the vista spreading below them. A sudden gust of wind swirled an eddy of dust across the slope directly below them. He turned to Catherine.

These sentences are used to break up the dialogue and remind the reader where the action is taking place, in this case in a cave high up on a barren mountainside.

A compelling storyline

There are some essential ingredients that go into writing a story that will be a compelling read.

Conflict

The driving force behind any story is conflict. Every scene that contains some sort of interaction between your characters should contain some sort of conflict. This doesn't mean the conflict has to be overt or violent – it can be subtle, and should relate to the overall theme of your memoir.

Goals

By this I don't mean your goals in writing your memoir, but rather the goals you, as the main character in your story, are trying to achieve. So, if you've been severely injured in an accident and left somewhat incapacitated as a result, your goals might be to overcome physical or mental challenges. Your readers will clearly empathise with you in this case and want you to achieve your goals.

Do you remember the hypothetical scenarios we looked at earlier, about your fictional World War II veteran father, and then your made-up life farming in a third-world country?

In scenario 1 your goal might be to survive your father's unreasonable, harsh and unrelenting attempts to make you into soldiers. This could be both funny and tragic as you come up with inventive ways to escape his tyranny and he defeats each one – until the tragic death of your brother.

In scenario 2 your goal might be to cope with the many challenges involved in farming and living in a third-world country.

Throughout your memoir, you, the main character, will be trying to achieve your goals and overcome any obstacles that are in the way of you achieving this.

Evolution

Readers find it easier to identify with characters that grow and change during the course of a story. So, taking the scenarios mentioned earlier, at the beginning of your memoir about your World War II father and his influence on your life you might start off as naïve, vulnerable, timid and nervous and gradually evolve through events that happen to you into a less naïve, less vulnerable, bold and assertive person who is able to take charge of his own life.

In scenario 2 you might begin the story as trusting, optimistic, a bit bombastic and enthusiastic, and as events unfold you become mistrustful, more guarded in your approach, a little cynical, but you remain optimistic and enthusiastic, even if this is somewhat tempered by what you have lived through. You may even emerge as someone suffering from post-traumatic stress and that may shape your sequel in your new country.

Suspense

Suspense is a product of posing questions which remain unanswered for as long as possible – Can she survive? Will he win? – and it's the most important facet of storytelling, because it's what keeps your reader turning the page. If you can, keep your readers guessing about the outcome of your story as much as you can.

Pace how you reveal information, and by this I mean don't give away too much too soon. Withhold answers to questions for as long as you reasonably can so that your reader has to wait with anticipation for the solution to be revealed. This all helps create or increase suspense.

A good ending

The ending of your memoir is an important part of your book as it will determine whether your reader then goes on to read other works you write. If you have a rushed or disappointing ending, your readers will be unlikely to read more of your work.

More of my work? you might ask. Well, yes. Writing memoir can become almost a compulsion and quite a few memoirists have gone on to write more than one memoir.

Some examples are, Frank McCourt, who wrote *Angela's Ashes* and its sequel, *'Tis;* Mandy Sayer, who wrote *Dreamtime Alice* and *The Poet's Wife*; and Alexandra Fuller, who has written a number of books, including two memoirs, *Don't Let's Go to the Dogs Tonight* and *Leaving Before the Rains Come*.

So don't discount that you might write more than one memoir.

But having a good ending doesn't only apply to your memoir as a whole. It also applies to each scene. While you are examining each scene, check to see you have ended it in such a way that your reader is compelled to move on to the next scene to find out what happens next. Cliff-hangers can be a really effective way to do this, but be careful not to overdo these as too many one after the other can become annoying. Try to achieve an intriguing ending while still not overusing any one method.

Dealing with writer's block

At some stage during the writing of your memoir you might find that you simply don't know how to continue and are unable to write, a situation often referred to as writer's block.

A common reason for writer's block is that you don't know enough about your subject, so you might need to do some research in order to carry on.

Otherwise, a way round this block when doing any kind of writing, whether it be memoir, non-fiction or fiction, is to make a mark, such as an asterisk, or put a note in brackets (research) and carry on writing. You can come back later when you've had a chance to do some research and fill in the blanks.

Another more complex reason for a period of writer's block might be because you have arrived at a passage in your life which is painful to recall and which you would rather not make public, but which you cannot ignore.

What should you do? Should you go ahead and include these incidences or leave them out?

The answer is that it's your memoir and it's up to you how much you reveal. If there are topics that you would rather not have the whole world know but you'd still like to write about to get them straight in your mind, then do so. Writing is as much a cathartic and healing process as it is art.

Try putting aside thoughts of publication and write about these memories, secure in the knowledge they will never be published. Even if you had no intention of attaining a global audience, resolve beforehand that this section will never be read by anyone else, and then write about these memories honestly, purging yourself of the painful recollections that are preventing you from telling the story you would like to tell.

Once you have dealt with these issues you will no doubt find you can continue with the rest of your memoir that you are comfortable having in the public domain.

Tip

Writing memoir or any good story is like laying a trail of crumbs for a bird. You lead the readers along, feeding them crumbs, keeping them following you as you reveal the story. Follow the principles of good storytelling and you won't go far wrong.

Summary

- Consider using a file for each character
- Ask yourself: Are you writing for publication, or are you writing for yourself, family or friends?
- Write chapters or anecdotes in any order you choose
- Make people feel emotion as they read
- Follow good storytelling principles, paying attention to the overall structure and components of a good story
- Deal with writer's block

Writing exercise 1:

Write at least half a page using the words 'The thing I don't want to write about is ...'

Writing exercise 2:

Read the following excerpt:

Mandy and I kept in touch every few days, back and forth across the Atlantic. As I sat with the phone pressed to my ear, staring at the shag-pile carpet between my feet, I imagined her in the dingy flat she'd managed to rent in London. She sounded sad and depressed, lonely and cold; and I felt obliged to play out my side of the drama.

I longed for the old times when Mandy and I would share some cheap wine, smoke weed and listen to Midnight Oil. But I knew those days were gone.

Late one night she rang – it would have been early morning for her, a time of bleak grey dawn lightening above the crowded row upon row of houses. She was crying and I waited, listening to the sounds of the unceasing New York traffic surging outside my window, while she sobbed into the phone. I had the receiver pressed hard against my ear and imagined myself holding her, her head tucked under my chin as I stroked her hair.

I love you, I said. We'll get through this. It's okay.

It isn't okay. It'll never be okay again. What we did was wrong.

Wrong? How could something that felt so right for me feel wrong to her? But I had to keep up my end of the bargain.

He would have had an awful life with us. It's better this way. He's gone to a loving home. Don't beat yourself up about it.

She sniffed into the phone. You didn't want him. I know that, and that's what hurts. He was a part of me, and it feels like you've rejected me along with him.

I wanted to throw the phone at the wall, yell, scream. We'd had this conversation so many times. Instead I gripped the phone tighter and forced myself to breathe calmly.

I don't have anyone to talk to, she wailed.

I gritted my teeth. What about me? I wanted to scream. Don't I count as someone? Obviously not. It wasn't that I didn't empathise with her. I did. But every time I'd considered the possibility of us raising a child together, the product of another man's seed – the product of her brutal rape – I just couldn't see myself doing it. Not successfully, anyway. No, it was better this way, even if we – us – didn't survive as a couple. The boy would be happier where he was, adopted out to a family who would love him and care for him untainted by knowledge of his conception.

In that I was wrong, of course, but I wasn't to know that until I met him after his eighteenth birthday.

Did you enjoy this piece?
If yes, then what did you enjoy about it?
If no, then what didn't you enjoy about it?

Write down what you can glean from this piece, such as who are the characters, how old are they, what are their social circumstances, what are they like, what are their likes and dislikes, what emotions do they feel, what is the relationship between the characters, what do you think might be happening, and where is this piece set? Go into plenty of detail and see how much you can surmise about the overall story.

Once you have done that, what I'd like you to note in the above piece is how this author has omitted quote marks from his dialogue. Did you like that or did you find it difficult to distinguish between dialogue and narration, or even his thoughts? Bear in mind that while this lack of conventional punctuation might work for established authors, it might not be okay if you want to land a deal with a traditional publisher.

Punctuation evolved to help make the meaning of any piece of writing clearer to the reader, so not using one of these very important tools might count against you.

Also note how he has handled setting and anchored his scene at various points by reminding us where the scene is set.

Another important point is how this author has handled the timeline. He has kept most of the scene immediate, as though it was happening right then, but then the last line skips forward in time and presages something awful that's lined up for the future. This poses questions in the reader's mind and adds to suspense and tension.

Writing exercise 3:

Try writing a story from your own life emulating how this story has been told.

Publishing Methods

So you've decided you would like to go public with your memoir. You would like anyone, anywhere, to be able to read what you have to say. Or perhaps you don't want all and sundry to read your work, but you would like a record of your life and views available to a select group. How do you go about doing this? There are a number of options.

Traditional

Many writers dream of a mega-million-dollar publishing deal once they've finished writing their book, but the sad fact is most books that are written will never be traditionally published, let alone be mainstream published. What do I mean by traditional and mainstream?

Traditional publishing means you will receive an advance against your future sales before the publishing house, whether it be big or small, publishes your book. The publisher will pay for all editing, cover design, book layout, marketing and so forth. All you need to do is bank the cheque. Mind you, these days even traditionally published authors have to do a lot of their own marketing. You should not be required to outlay any money in order for your book to be published, apart from the time you have spent researching, writing and editing it.

Mainstream publishing encompasses all of the above but means that you have scored a deal with one of the big and established publishing houses, such as Penguin Random House, Pan Macmillan, HarperCollins, Schuster & Schuster, etc.

I must warn you that trying to be traditionally published is a very hard path to take, especially if you have written a memoir. This doesn't mean it's impossible, just that there are a lot of well-written, interesting manuscripts out there, and unless you're famous or infamous you're unlikely to attract a traditional publishing deal.

There are famous exceptions, of course, such as *Angela's Ashes* and *'Tis* by Frank McCourt; or *Dreamtime Alice* and *The Poet's Wife* by Mandy Sayer; *Don't Let's Go to the Dogs Tonight* and *Leaving Before the Rains Come* by Alexandra Fuller; and *Mao's Last Dancer* by Li Cunxin; as well as many others.

Self-publishing

There are plenty of companies online who can help you through this process or you can go it alone. Self-publishing can be both rewarding and daunting. Many people are going that route, though, so it's definitely an option worth considering.

If you decide not to use a self-publishing company and would rather do the work yourself then make sure you do a really professional job. The reading public is picky and a poorly written, poorly edited and badly laid out book is likely to turn off potential readers.

Beta readers

My advice is to use a number of beta readers to give you feedback on the content of your book. Beta readers are not editors or proof-readers, although those who offer their services often do have these skills as well. This is not their function, however. They are there to test your book for readability, to help you pick up flaws in the plot, in consistency, in pacing.

Plot? you might say. This is a memoir. It has no plot.

That's true to an extent, but if you're aiming for a wide readership then your memoir will have a storyline. It will have a structure similar to the plot in a novel.

You may find it difficult to find beta readers for a memoir but try looking online. There are web sites dedicated to putting authors and beta readers together, and there are groups on sites such as Goodreads dedicated to this as well.

I have read it's often best to get as many as twenty beta readers for your book before self-publishing it, but in practice it's really hard to find that many. You'll also find opinions vary widely so you'll need to sift through the feedback to find common threads that could indicate potential weaknesses and then work on those. You'll need to develop a thick skin as well.

Manuscript assessors

Once you have finished writing your memoir, you might like to send it to a paid manuscript assessor. There are plenty of assessors out there, and if you can't find one online then try asking at your local library for writing groups in your area. Members of these groups might be able to recommend an assessor, or if your state or region has an overall body which helps writers they should be able to give you a comprehensive list.

If you join groups on Goodreads, though, you should be able to ask other writers in the groups who they would recommend.

To recap thus far, the process is: write your memoir; check it thoroughly yourself, reading it aloud to pick up any faults; send it to a paid professional manuscript assessor; or send it to at least three beta readers (more if you can find them). You may like to use both a paid assessor and beta readers.

Editors

Once you're happy your book is as good as it can be, send it to a professional editor who will go through it with a fine-tooth comb and pick up any remaining inconsistencies in the plot or characters, any grammatical errors, spelling mistakes, typos etc.

This is an important step, so don't be tempted to skimp on it and it's essential if you want to sell your books on Smashwords and Amazon. Your memoir won't make it into Smashwords' premium catalogue if it's full of mistakes.

If you're not sure where to find an editor then use a search engine and type in 'professional book editor'. If you live in Australia then all states have a Society of Editors, and I'm sure this will apply to most countries around the world.

If you would rather deal with someone who is recommended, then try asking at your local library, or ask at a local writers' group, writers' society, or book club. There is also a host of groups on sites such as Goodreads where you can post a topic to find an editor or ask others to recommend someone to you.

Cover design

While the book is being edited, you can start to look around for someone to design a really great cover for you.

This is another point where it's worth spending money for a really professional job. Most books only appear as a thumbnail in catalogues or online these days so the cover must be eye-catching and appealing, and the font for the title and author must be easily readable.

If you don't know a graphic designer, try looking on sites such as 99Designs, Bespoke Book Covers, Spiffing Covers, and UpWork. Goodreads also has a group dedicated to book cover designers and book illustrators so you'll be spoilt for choice. Smashwords has a list of cover designers for ebooks. It's a free list and it's up to you to check out the artist's work and then contact them. Prices vary, but they're not expensive.

Once again, it's as well to ask around and get a personal recommendation before embarking on such an important step. If you're using an individual, at least check out the artist's portfolio, and if you're using a site, then read plenty of reviews before employing an artist via the site.

Many of the sites which help you publish your book yourself will also have cover designers associated with them, so have a look at what's offered by Amazon, Feedaread and Smashwords. Some of the artists charge very little for an ebook cover. Print covers cost more because they're more complicated.

You will need to know the final page count of the book before the graphic designer can finalise the print version cover of your book. This obviously does not apply for ebooks.

In your brief, ask for multiple versions of the cover design. You'll need a .pdf file for print, and .jpeg or .png files, or both, for loading onto web sites for promotions, plus various front cover files for uploading to sites like Kindle Direct Publishing, Smashwords, Lightning Source, and Lulu.

If you have great graphic design skills and would like to do the cover yourself, then you can download cover templates from Createspace and Lightning Source, and you can buy stock photos online at sites such as Shutterstock, iStockphoto, Getty Images, Fotolia, Dreamstime, Free Digital Photos, Depositphotos, and Bigstockphoto. These sites also apply if you need to buy stock photos for your chosen graphic designer to use.

Book layout

If you can't do the interior book layout yourself, employ someone who can. Once they have finished their work, they should provide you with a number of files, including a .pdf for the print version, plus suitable ebook versions to upload to sites such as Kindle Direct Publishing and Smashwords. These are usually done in Word. At the time of writing, Smashwords requires the .doc versions of Word files, not .docx. KDP can handle .pdf files, but this is not advised. It's better to follow the site's guidelines to make sure you do a really professional job.

For print layout, Createspace will do the whole job for you, at a price, and Lightning Source has a list of people they recommend, but there are lots of people who can do this type of layout as well, so do an online search, or find someone via word of mouth.

Proofreading

Before uploading your .pdf file or your Word files, proof them really carefully. You might like to get a professional proof-reader to check them as well. Proofing doesn't cost as much as editing. If you feel you can't afford this step then by all means get someone else to proof your book for you. You can do it yourself, but you'll find that a fresh set of eyes makes a big difference. Others who are unfamiliar with our work pick up faults our eyes tend to skip over.

Once the book has been published, it's still advisable to thoroughly proof the book. Mistakes can creep in despite your best efforts. Check that the layout is correct and re-read your work or get someone else to read it to make sure there are no errors.

This sounds like a lot of hassle, but it's definitely worth it to produce a top-quality book.

Print on demand

Again, there are hosts of companies that provide a print-on-demand service. Probably most notable amongst them now is Lightning Source. The beauty is that many of these POD versions offer worldwide distribution and that means one of the big hurdles to self-publishing has been removed. Feedaread, Lulu and Createspace, the print arm of Amazon, also do POD, but there are plenty of others out there.

Please bear in mind that any photos you include in your book will appear as black and white unless you go for one of the specialty books, which can be prohibitively expensive, depending on how many photos you include, how big your book is, and who you use.

Print on demand is becoming more and more popular, and with good reason. It means you don't have boxes and boxes of books lying around unsold and unread. I know of one person who, some years ago, ordered her print books and they took up the space of a large four-wheel-drive.

Blogs

If you just want to get your story out there almost as a journal with photos then a blog might be for you.

It can act as a diary or journal, and if you keep records of what goes on your blog then you will leave a great history for your family and friends to look back on. It's also a good way to gauge how much interest there is in what you're writing about.

A friend of mine posted interesting articles and photos when she did a recent year-long trip around Australia. As the expedition was likely to be a once-off, she geared the blog specifically to that experience. Don't expect an instant following. It can take a while to build. At first she had only a few followers, but these grew during the course of the year and beyond as people from all over the world tuned in for more information about travelling around Australia.

You could gear your blog to family history and stories about family members, or to a particular incident in your life, such as a memorable sojourn you spent in a foreign country – anything that takes your fancy and you'd like the rest of the world to know about.

If you would rather keep this for a closed circle, then it is possible to stipulate that your blog will be private and you can invite people to view it. I'm not an expert on computer or web security, but I would advise that you still be circumspect about what you post and assume that the content of the blog could become public knowledge.

Examples of blog hosts are Blogspot and Wordpress, amongst others.

Ebooks

Ebooks are one of the most exciting innovations to hit publishing in recent decades. Many companies now offer conversion of your files to a digital format or ebook, and you can get one done and published on free sites such as Smashwords and Amazon's Kindle Direct Publishing very easily. Lightning Source and Blurb also offer ebook conversion, but there are others as well.

If you would rather do the conversion yourself, you'll find that many of the modern word-processing programs offer conversion to both .epub (able to be read on most ereaders, including Kindle) and .mobi (able to be read on Kindle only).

The beauty of using sites such as Smashwords, Kindle Direct, and Lightning Source is that they also offer worldwide distribution, which is a massive bonus and removes what used to be one of the major impediments to self-publishing or indie publishing.

An added advantage is that you can still have illustrations or photos in your ebook. A word of warning here: formatting your ebook requires painstaking attention to detail. Formatting your ebook with photos or illustrations requires even more painstaking attention to detail and can be a frustrating experience. However, if you want good results, you do need to pay this attention to detail.

If you're not sure you can manage the ebook layout yourself then there are individuals and companies who will do this for you for a fee. Smashwords has a list of people who will do the layout for you at affordable prices, otherwise check with your editor or layout person to see if they can do ebook layout or know someone who can.

With Smashwords, once you get into the premium catalogue, your ebook will go to all the major online retailers.

Both Smashwords and Kindle Direct offer free style guides to help you format your work, and they also offer advice on marketing either online or via free books or articles.

As mentioned before, your memoir will no doubt contain some photos, so a word of warning here is that photos don't always behave as you would expect them to. I've had problems when using photos in ebooks uploaded to Smashwords, despite following their guidelines. In my experience, though, Kindle Direct Publishing has no problem including the photos, although it's as well to keep in mind that on some devices the photos will appear in black and white, while on others they will be in colour.

Caution

The hardest part of publishing at the moment is marketing, and with all these methods mentioned above, the marketing is either entirely or mostly still up to you. It's best to have realistic expectations about sales. Your books may not sell at all or you may sell only five or ten. It depends on how good the story is and how good your marketing is.

Private

If you decide you'd rather not make your work public then another option besides going print-on-demand is to keep the book entirely private and maybe just print off a few copies for family and friends. You can buy inexpensive ring binders to bind the books at home, or you can go to a place that will do the binding for you. There are a number of options available, such as perfect binding, wire spiral binding and plastic spiral binding.

Audio books

An exciting development on the audio front is the possibility of converting your story into an audio book, so you could conceivably have your memoir available in print, as an ebook, and also as an audio book. Amazon definitely offers a facility to convert your file into an audio book, so check out their site if this interests you.

Photo books

This is an exciting innovation that has been made possible in the last decade, and it's opened up a whole new world for people wanting to write their life story.

There are various commercial enterprises that offer affordable means to create and then print one-off photo albums for occasions such as weddings and special anniversaries, but these could also be used to document your life pictorially, focusing on those scenes which mean most to you. A good number of these albums allow you to say a few words about each photo, but those I've had experience with don't allow you substantial quantities of text.

A way around this is to create a book using a word processing program and then insert photos into the book in the appropriate place. You'll probably want to include photos in your memoir anyway, even if it's mostly text.

A downside of including too many photos in the past is that these books, if they included colour photos, were really expensive to print – prohibitively so.

The good news is that now most print-on-demand companies already mentioned allow you to print books with colour photos at a much more affordable price than was the case previously.

However, if the cost of printing the books is still too expensive for you, then you could of course just keep these books as a computer file or in any one of the manners already described.

If you do decide to go ahead with making your book generally available, though, you aren't restricted to printed versions. You could put your picture book onto a memory stick or disk.

You could also try making your photo memoir into an .epub or .mobi ebook, but at the moment this is fraught with difficulties. Technology is changing all the time, though, and if there's a demand for photo memoirs as this type of ebook then I'm sure someone somewhere will find a way round the difficulties.

If you decide to make a family photo book or album, then try sites such as Blurb, Vistaprint, Snapfish, Milkbooks, Memento, Shutterfly, Artisan State, and Mixbook. The albums can be really classy, from soft covers to hard covers with linen or leather finishes. If you don't like any of the above sites, an internet search will turn up many others.

If you don't want to make it so formal you could still make up an album of photos that mean a lot to you. You could then write a caption or longer piece about each photo, and the end result would be a pictorial history for your family to follow.

If you're able to scan photos into your computer, or you already have digital images, then you can still produce a great book – and it doesn't have to be expensive. You could produce and print a few copies for your family – the number is up to you – and then produce a .pdf file which people could store on their computers or on their ereaders.

Converting your file to a .pdf is easy to do these days. If you use Word then just choose 'save as' and scroll down to 'pdf'. (A word of warning is that this method of conversion will not suffice when converting a file to .pdf for a print version of a book to be published; for that you will need specialist software. If you don't have the correct software and are loath to buy it then try downloading a free .pdf converter from the web or ask someone else to do the conversion for you.)

Pdf files can, for instance, be emailed to family overseas. Keep in mind that too many photos may make the book hard for your recipients to download.

Making backups

If you decide that you'd really rather not go to the trouble of printing out copies of your life story, or having it formatted into a book for yourself or a publisher, then you can still write it and keep it on your computer, on an external hard drive, memory stick, CD or DVD, or in a cloud. (Storing your work on a cloud can be as simple as emailing the file to yourself.)

However, I would still advise that you print out at least one copy in case your file is destroyed or becomes corrupted or technology changes so much that it's no longer accessible.

It would be a shame for your life story to be lost.

Summary

The following are all methods you might like to consider to immortalise your memoir. You might like to use one or a number of different methods; there's no hard and fast rule.

- A traditional publishing deal
- Self-publishing
- Print on demand
- Writing a blog
- Creating an ebook
- Creating an audio book
- Creating a photo book or a photo album
- Don't forget to back up your memoir

Writing exercise 1:

Write a 500-word back cover blurb for your memoir. Make it a marketing pitch that will attract readers and don't forget to seamlessly include key words that people are likely to use when doing a search online. What is it about your memoir that will attract readers?

Once you have done that then try honing the 500 words down to only one paragraph of no more than three or four sentences.

Now try honing your blurb down even further, to only one sentence. This will be your 'elevator pitch', the one you will bring out when anyone asks what your memoir is about.

Writing exercise 2:

Write a 500-word synopsis of your memoir. The aim of a synopsis is to give an overall view of what your story is about and it uses 'telling' rather than 'showing'. Usually literary agents or publishers or looking for a story arc, so they want to see if your memoir is well developed with a beginning, middle and end, and whether it has a theme that will appeal to readers.

Once you have finished your 500-word synopsis, try cutting this down to only one paragraph and then further refine it to only one sentence.

Writing exercise 3:

Write a covering letter to an agent or publisher. Keep it brief, but include your brief one-sentence pitch from exercise 1, the working title and word count of your memoir, and then detail any previous publication successes you have had, or what made you decide to write this memoir in the first place. Is it like any movies or TV series you have seen? Then mention these too.

Do one online search for prospective agents and/or publishers. Read their submission guidelines and, once you have done this, practise tailoring your covering letter to fit their criteria.

Building a Family Tree

Having a family tree at the back or front of your memoir is often a good idea as this enables anyone who reads your book to understand where various characters fit in. If you don't already have one then there are a number of ways this can be done.

If you do a search online you'll find a host of web sites that offer family tree templates. Try MyHeritage; Ancestry.com, and its variations; Legacy Family Tree; Geni.com; Lucidchart; Tribal Pages; and Findmypast.

Should you not be all that confident using a computer program, you can draw up a tree of your own, using one of these methods.

1. Alice Blogs married (2) Douglas Person

    1.1   Sarah Person (born 1900)

    1.2   Julia Person (born 1901)

    1.3   Alfred Person (born 1903)

    1.4   John Person (born 1910)

1.1   Sarah Person married William Man

    1.1.1   Charles Man (born 1923)

    1.1.2   Lucy Man (born 1926)

1.2   Julia Person married Egbert Bloke

    1.2.1   Gilbert Bloke (born 1924)

    1.2.2   Hugh Bloke (born 1926)

1.3   Alfred Person married Anne Lady

    1.3.1   Lucy Lady (born 1933)

    1.3.2   Florence Lady (born 1935)

1.4   John Person (died in infancy)

You could do a number of charts this way. For instance, those labelled 1 would list everyone who is related to the Blogs family, while those labelled 2 would list everyone who is related to the Person family. You can even colour-code them to make the charts easier to understand, Blogs in red and Person in blue, for instance.

You could also draw up a chart using blocks for your ancestors' names and then have lines or arrows to them to show who married whom and who their children are. These are best done in a landscape format so that you can fit as much information as possible on a page.

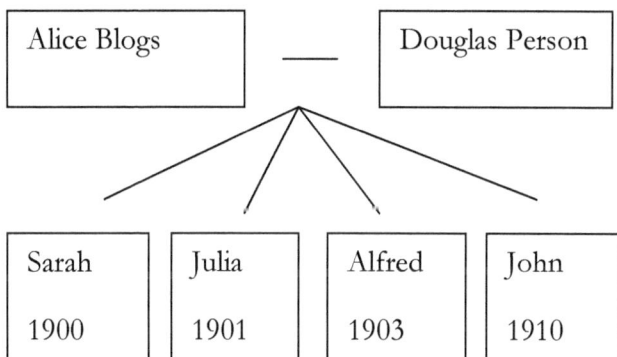

| Alice Blogs | ___ | Douglas Person |

| Sarah 1900 | Julia 1901 | Alfred 1903 | John 1910 |

Conclusion

Above all else, while at times recalling memories will make you laugh and some will make you cry, I hope writing your memoir will be an enjoyable and rewarding experience, something that leaves you feeling fulfilled rather than drained. Overall, keep in mind your ultimate objective: to leave a lasting legacy of your life. I hope that you will find it liberating, cathartic, and fun.

If you found this book helpful, please consider writing a review on the site where you bought it and/or on Goodreads. Reviews are really helpful to authors and readers alike. If you feel like contacting me, please do.

My email address is kathystewart640@gmail.com.

I'd love to hear from you.

Acknowledgements

No book is ever written in isolation and I'd like to thank all those who have helped me with the production of this one, either by giving me much needed advice, or by reading the content with a critical eye, or by teaching me about writing memoir via their manuscripts. I've learnt much from the authors whose books I've worked on, and it's always been a pleasure to offer advice and see your books take shape. Thanks to the members of the writing groups I belong to for the critical eye you cast over my work. Thanks too to my sisters who have helped with my own family research and who have always been valuable and fun partners in crime.

Useful Sites

Please note, this list of useful sites is by no means comprehensive, but it should help set you on the right track to find the information you need. I haven't listed any sites for non-English-speaking countries, or even for all English-speaking countries, but the same search principles apply worldwide.

USA

National Archives and Records Administration:
www.archives.gov and www.usa.gov
The National Museum of the United States Army:
https://armyhistory.org
National Museum of American History:
http://americanhistory.si.edu/
Gettysburg National Military Park:
www.nps.gov/gett
National Military History Center:
www.nationalmilitaryhistorycenter.org
Library of Congress: www.loc.gov

Smithsonian National Museum of Natural History: http://www.mnh.si.edu/

UK

The National Archives:

www.nationalarchives.gov.uk and

https://www.gov.uk

Imperial War Museums: www.iwm.org.uk

The British Library: www.bl.uk

British Museum: www.britishmuseum.org

CANADA

Library and Archives Canada: www.bac-lac.gc.ca

Canadian War Museum: www.warmuseum.ca

AUSTRALIA

National Archives of Australia: www.naa.gov.au

Australian War Memorial: https://www.awm.gov.au

National Library of Australia: www.nla.gov.au

National Museum of Australia: www.nma.gov.au

SOUTH AFRICA

National Archives of South Africa:

www.national.archives.gov.za

South African National Museum of Military History:

www.ditsong.org.za

National Library of South Africa: www.nlsa.ac.za

South African Museum: www.iziko.org.za